After Trump:
How Nationalism
Can Save America

Tom Kawczynski

Copyright © 2018 by Tom Kawczynski

All rights reserved. This book or any portion thereof may not be reproduced or used in any manner whatsoever without the express written permission of the author except for the use of brief quotations in a book review.

Printed in the United States of America

First Printing, 2018

Contents

Introduction 4

Chapter 1: Trump – A Singular Talent 14

Chapter 2: The GOP Must Be More Than Economics 24

Chapter 3: The GOP Must Fight the Culture War with Equal Force 36

Chapter 4: Smaller Government Isn't Always Better. 47

Chapter 5: Nationalism's Beginnings – Laws and Symbols 58

Chapter 6: Forging Nationalism - Slow Road to Culture 70

Chapter 7: Nationalism Realized – How Identity Becomes Ethnicity 82

Chapter 8: The Values that Build a Nation 94

Chapter 9: Immigration – A Country Is Its People 104

Chapter 10: Family Planning – Children are the Future 114

Chapter 11: Culture and Education – Too Important to Ignore 124

Chapter 12: Foreign Disentanglement Guarantees Independence 134

Chapter 13: Rebuilding America - Systems for Success 144

Chapter 14: Finance – Take Back Our Money 154

Chapter 15: Next Steps 164

Chapter 16: The Price of Failure 179

Epilogue 187

Acknowledgments 190

Introduction

The Election of Donald Trump as the 45th President of the United States is the inflection point upon which our future rests. His victory has exposed the rot at the core of our republic, and has shown the rabid Left to be an angry mob threatening the destruction of our entire country. Though we are enjoying economic success, such success is only escalating the cultural conflict. This forces us to ask what we can do now, during his presidency, and we must also ask: "What comes after Trump?"

How do we fix this mess? People's greatest concern once they become aware of all that has happened in America, and how our civilization literally rests on a knife's edge, is figuring out how we can walk ourselves back from the abyss.

My first two books cover the deceptions by which our past was unmade (*Someone Has to Say It: The Hidden History of How America Was Lost*), and our present peril with these gaping social divisions (*The Coming Civil War*) and will provide invaluable background for understanding the content of this text. If you have either read these books or kept yourself well-informed, you know that the only realistic position is to admit at the outset that setting our nation on a path to future success is an uncertain road at best.

The feel-good moment we are enjoying under President Trump, while a much needed and well-earned respite, has thus far failed to deal with the three primary problems that are unmaking America. These are:

1) The Deep State continues to hold significant power, working across different nations to impact global events, especially in the Western World, and to public appearances, has successfully managed to distract and divert the Trump Presidency.

2) The demographic replacement of the White majority in America, which is the bulwark of the voting population who support traditional values and functionally serve as the guarantors of the liberties specified in the Constitution continues, although slowed by reductions in refugee and immigration admissions.

3) The primary sources of cultural transmission remain hostile to the historical majority of American citizens as they have been for decades, working to actively undermine confidence in our nation, sow constant division, and through their control of education, radicalize upcoming generations against the surviving order.

These are not issues which will be solved by one administration or even in one generation. Progress is certainly being made during the Trump Administration, and there are emerging hints and glimmers that more is happening behind the scenes to redress these pressing concerns. We, the general public, cannot fully know the extent of these actions, even as we hope and pray they succeed to their fullest potential.

While retaining optimism, and ensuring the efforts being made by this administration continue to receive our warranted support, especially when attacking these sensitive areas, it is our task to ensure that what is happening now is the beginning of a new epoch in America's history rather than the last celebration of a soon-to-be-transformed America fading into history. Toward this end we must plan, organize, and act to push policies that directly deal with the challenges above.

This is going to get ugly. Even the best-case scenario wherein we fight to unmake the corruption of the Deep State, implement a sane immigration policy that puts America and the current American citizenry first, and we rebuild a healthy culture that has been deliberately shattered into pain and deception, our efforts are going to force conflict to the center of national debate. Those who push the ideas we oppose are not doing so by accident, but rather as part of a decades old effort to sow division in such way that the American people surrender our civilization and our nation to their control.

A few years ago, most decent people who lean right of center would have struggled to accept the notion that common-sense political reforms would trigger conflict but consider the Kavanaugh hearings which happened the month before I began this text as a textbook case. Before the nominee was even selected, every member of the institutional Left, both inside and outside government signaled their opposition. Once Kavanaugh stepped into the hot seat, he was subject to outrageous, unsubstantiated, and injurious claims that represented the worst slander and libel imaginable against a man and his family. The sole purpose of that slander was to destroy him. The media, far from making any pretenses of objectivity or even requiring evidence, served as the henchmen to rally the beat mob.

All men were blamed. All Whites were blamed. Civility was discarded as people were attacked in public for offering dissent and taking the once shared position that simply accusing a man of a criminal act, absent any corroborating evidence or testimony, was insufficient to render judgment. The Left accepts this because they have long since decided that anyone who offers up a defense of our civilization, as Justice Kavanaugh did in his spirited personal defense and through a lifetime's service to the rule of law, is their enemy.

They consider the destruction of those of us who defend America as it was to be virtuous, and while sorry paeans will be heard about how the passions of the moment have temporarily made these otherwise decent people forget themselves, don't believe that lie for one second. They knew what they were doing, from the Feinstein leaks, to the New Yorker stories, to creepy porn lawyers like Avenatti and group rape stories made up in Rhode Island. They have always believed that the ends justify the means, and should we be so foolish as to return power to them, we would – as President Trump rightly states – be giving matches to the arsonists.

The sorry truth is that identity politics are here to stay. Republicans and decent folk imagine that if sufficient opportunity were granted to the groups who make up the Left then people would walk away from their lunacy and see the opportunities that have been before them, more now than ever. Some certainly will do just that, and we should welcome them into the fold as their awakening comes. But we must also be realistic and recognize that if for each person saved another fifty remain lost and even more belligerent, we cannot keep policy moving forward with a virtuous few striving against the angry mob. Those who cannot be saved must be put down. This is a bitter pill, but also a political reality which if ignored threatens our own survival.

Operating from this realistic premise, this book endeavors to ask where we should go after Trump, and how we will solve these problems in the most humane yet effective manner possible. Striking the right balance between these approaches will be hellishly difficult, especially as it must be done in the face of what will likely become increasingly violent opposition. But the question is worth asking for the generations who gave their work, effort, and even their lives to build this country. We must be better than those we face, but we cannot be pushovers anymore.

Now we enter an age where hard moral questions must be asked once more that will offend and wound people, including good folk who are our friends. We've had the bad habit for far too long of avoiding unpleasant questions that needed to be answered, turning indifference into the false virtue of tolerance, and allowing the lunatics to run the asylum so long as we could keep them off our lawns and penned in a place where the harm they can do to themselves or others are minimized. We surrendered our values, our institutions, most of our cities, and much of our government, and almost all our schools on this basis, and now we face an angry colossus that is but a generation away from realizing their nihilistic plot to destroy America.

We can only fix this if our people come together in opposition to these ideas, and if we have the gumption to recognize that the people unwilling to fight these battles are no longer our people. When reason fails to persuade, and violence is threatened against us, we have no choice but to act pro-actively in defense of our folk, our values, and our heritage. We must be willing to fight with the same passion and ardor in preservation of the good America we love that they are willing to exert in unmaking this America they so clearly hate and despise.

We must accept the fact now that we cannot save everyone, or this book will be lost upon you. We will all lose friends and people dear to us in the forthcoming struggle, but the longer we delay and the more meekly we proceed, the greater those losses will be, not just among our opponents, but among our own ranks of the good people who are willing to fight these battles.

Maybe this conflict is a bit personal for me because I live the reality of a good man being unjustly slandered for loving my people, and then having to watch people I know to agree with me pretend to look away and disown me because they didn't want to face this monstrosity. Such cowardice is unseemly, but the habit of the age. How many more times will we sacrifice our own upon the altar of political correctness, to values we know to be false, for the cause of peace? Patrick Henry spoke well enough about the cost of such surrender, and our Founders knew times would come when we would have to fight for our values and the cost would be high – higher still with any delays with which we proceed, and should we fail to stand in mutual support of one another and our core values.

Now that the stakes are understood, take a breath with me, and let's put our reason to work to try to figure out the best-case scenario we can create. There is much cause for hope in that nationalism has never been more popular, that at the moment the Right controls all but one of the elected branches of the government, that the Left is revealing their wicked debasement prematurely, and that good people have more tools today to communicate and collaborate than in any time in human history. What has been lacking is honesty about the problems we face and the will to deal with these firmly. Exercise of both honesty and will in the present, though having costs of their own, could mitigate the worst problems later.

This book opens with three big areas to think about in how we need to adapt our thinking to the future to be able to overcome the clear and present danger.

We need to understand why old models of the Right failed to prevent the Left from turning so many people against America. Why didn't wealth calm their anger? Why haven't our moral institutions survived? Was arguing for smaller government a strategic mistake? Did we act too much on principles and without enough pragmatism? Republicans cared too much about power and conservatives cared too much about being right to get their hands dirty – we must change that to compete against people whose amorality is their defining trait, or all will be lost.

Is nationalism the alternative? Considering how we see that our nation is clearly torn into two or more segments, with visions incoherent and incompatible with one another polluting the entire public discourse, does it not seem now that we need to forge some unifying basis upon which America is to endure if we hope to survive as anything more than a legal despotism? Is the civic nationalist pageantry of symbols and laws enough? Can we build culture anew from this point? On what basis is someone American, and can we become one people again? Let's go there.

What values are so important to us that we dare not put any price on them? What values can we trade, and upon which recognize intellectual diversity and freedom of opportunity that justifies this awful struggle ahead? I can't remember the last time anyone in politics seriously discussed why we put prices on some things, but not on others, and we aren't allowed to have social discussions about what is good because the very idea of virtue itself has been targeted for immolation. We need to ask what is healthy, what is priceless, and what is good again.

We need to answer these questions. Before we answer them, we need the courage to ask them, and to be sincere enough to recognize we may not like the answers, and it may put us into some uncomfortable places. As someone who lives in that ugly space between the tactful things we say as lies to keep civility and the uncouth truths whose denial is destroying us, I implore you to join the ranks of people who must seek the truth and speak it. Because without this, we have no hope of a mostly peaceful restoration. Because we cannot build a stable future on a foundation of lies.

With truth to guide us on the search for virtue, a journey whose path is almost always more valuable than the destination, we can look at policy pragmatically and ask what is needed to fix these problems. Severe sickness often calls for bitter pills, and what I will suggest here goes far beyond what we've considered having government do for generations. But, for all the hesitation people will feel – and with just cause based upon historical understanding of the dangers of using government to solve social problems – my impression is people on the Right share the awareness that we must work now to restore our culture and rebuild the bedrock foundations that once sustained both our physical and moral character. Given the choice between the exploitation the Left will offer through their control, and the alternative we might create to oppose them, I would bet upon our ability to get things right enough. We cannot let our fear of failure and the dangers of corruption with which future generations will inevitably have to contend scare us into surrendering our opportunity and responsibility to do something better now to reverse this long retreat. The time to act is now.

We close with a plan, recognizing those things we absolutely must do to have a chance to build upon the bridgehead Trump has opened for us, grateful for his leadership and courage, but recognizing that the responsibility for a better America must ultimately rest with We, the people, working to perfect this union against our own petty tyrants. We know what cannot be permitted, and we must begin discussing all else, in order to find a path so that good men and women might enjoy this nation – reforged more strongly than ever after defeating this adversity – and that we might endure still by the grace of God and in future peace and prosperity.

Should we fail to act boldly, I know not the particulars of how things will play out, but it is clear that there will be many dark days between now and any opportunity to reclaim what we will have surrendered. And we should be honest about that, because those who refuse to fight now for fear of their own inadequacy – be it moral, financial, social, or physical – those who see these struggles yet avert their gaze, are cowards. We need some courage, and even if you have just a little bit to give, every man or woman can speak out for truth and goodness, and we need us all. So, it begins…

Chapter 1: Trump – A Singular Talent

Trump is a throwback.

I believe the secret to understanding the Trump Presidency is that he represents the ideals of an older era. He is the epitome of the 1950's ideals in many ways – back before America was torn apart by cultural, racial, and social conflict. He is a throwback to a time when gender roles were well understood, and the values of Heritage America were considered much more universal. Make America Great Again calls upon a nostalgic vision seeking to restore American growth and prestige, believing that inspiration and industry are enough to bring our country back from the dark places we now tread.

It is a beginning, and an important beginning for which all of us on the Right ranging from moderates to radicals should be grateful. Our system had become so corrupt that it literally took a billionaire to overcome the challenges of the institutional parties and the corporate media to offer a populist appeal to the millions of Americans who have been waiting for someone to represent their interests. The ideal of America – work hard, earn honest pay, and enjoy your family has never gone away, but that understanding has never been put under more pressure than it is today. People were working harder for less, in jobs that didn't build anything other than ideas and interest, and the very value and utility of families were being questioned.

The Left was in the triumphal stages of what we might call their war against reality, where they began by unmaking cultural institutions and have since advanced to unmaking liberty, language, and law in order to create a world where up is down and girls are boys. I use that example because it demonstrates the division at the heart of our society. People on the Left genuinely believe that if a fifty-year old man feels he has the heart of a seven-year old girl, it's healthy to indulge his subjective reality, or what sane people would call a fantasy, and allow him to sit in the bathroom and play with other girls. Those of us who haven't become so abstracted from the true nature of things realize that such a man is likely to be the very pedophile from which we need to protect our daughters, because we still have concern for our children's well-being.

Trump understands these conflicts, and he jumped in as the voice of reason against an insane movement that was trying to unmake all that was good in America on the premise they could then introduce different values in replacement. In reality, the Left constantly changes and contradicts values, like how they manage to have gays in the same coalition with the Muslims who would glibly toss them from roofs, because they do not so much seek moral outcomes as they seek to destroy any alternative authority to the state. Their moral compass points only in one direction: Toward power and their sick dream to achieve ultimate equality by taking away from others any ability to resist. It's no accident every socialist country eventually succumbs either to full communism or a petty despot, because in the absence of value, people lose a sense of themselves and only follow the orders of those who threaten them.

Our current President succeeds by highlighting these contradictions, essentially calling out not just the ideology of the Leftists, but their most prominent voices in institutions like the media and the Democrat Party for stage managing this charade. How can they claim to be pro-American when they care more about the rights of illegals convicted of crimes in the United States than American citizens? How can they be patriots if they're more inclined to celebrate trampling our flag than venerating the sacrifices made on its behalf? How can they promote social justice when they believe accusations based solely on the basis of the identity of the accuser rather than seeking the facts of the case? Trump not only recognizes these fallacies, but he calls them out on their lies with such frankness and humor that it destroys the whole facade upon which their unreality rests.

Perhaps it is ironically appropriate that Trump's name is so like a trumpet because he is serving as a wakeup call to millions of Americans who were sleepwalking toward an abyss, not realizing that with our schools and media already turned against this nation and its historic intent, that the demographic transformation happening as we speak thanks to absurd immigration policies have the Left just a few terms in power from realizing a seismic shift whereby they can gain through numbers what they never could win through honest argument and debate. Now, the Right is awake, and we opened our eyes together to a reality where we cannot let them have power back, because to do so would be to submit ourselves into being the new criminals for our future masters. Our crime, to the Left, is our existence, and they sincerely hate us for our virtues and our simple assertion that sometimes A is better than B.

Our President is the poster child for excellence, to such a degree that sometimes I think he even knows how hyperbolic his actions seem, but like a true showman he plays to the cameras. He used the media's inability to resist controversy to disrupt the entire system, and through the most adroit sleight of hand I've ever seen in either a politician or statesman, he keeps the eyes of the socialists clearly fixated on their own petulant outrage whereby they reveal themselves and their true agenda. We know Trump knows he does this because he even admitted years before his election that his social media had become so powerful, he could make his enemies tell the truth. He has done that, and every day where he goes and speaks truth, more of America awakens to the lies they were spouting, and more people get the courage to speak truth in their own lives.

The awakening has begun, but our journey has truly just begun because even as we now enjoy the resurgence of American exceptionalism – the belief we are a people on a mission who have something excellent to accomplish, we also understand that our enemy is within. We see the unrepentant corruption of much of the bureaucracy, who believe their will should override that of the people, and their corporate and media allies who still hold so many of our people in bondage through ignorance and propaganda. We see the division being fostered in our country, and we know that many who oppose us do so because they have bad information, and yet we must still deal with those who push these conflicts and try to act humanely to those who are misguided.

And herein lies the weakness of Trump. His love for this country is so great that he will devote all his efforts to rescuing any who might be saved, and as a result he restrains himself from taking those actions which might be necessary to ensure we don't all go down. A committed civic nationalist, he has deliberately adopted the most universal form of national engagement to reach the broadest potential audience, hoping to convert people who've been beaten down over many years through not just promises, but an emerging economic reality that allows much more opportunity. It is an optimistic vision that deserves to succeed, but I regret that history is replete with examples of leaders who, because they wanted to do too much, ultimately failed due to overreach.

To be specific with respect to this book, what I'm suggesting is that Trump is trying very hard to bridge the cultural gaps, cultivated heavily along racial lines by the Left by bringing minorities into the Republican coalition he has forged, which is basically centrist on social welfare but harder right on immigration. From a purely moral perspective, the Right would have required such action to be taken before we went down the road of opposing the Left on the identarian basis I argue will become inevitable. But what Trump is doing is identifying those who want to assimilate to our historic values of industry, opportunity, and fairness, and welcoming them into the tent, hoping that enough people will switch to shift the culture for good.

Count me as a skeptic, not because Trump is wrong in his aspirations or because he will fail to attain some of them, but because of how tantalizing the promises of guilt and redistribution are, and how the Left manages to organize their core believers against the Right. As strange as it might sound, when times of prosperity emerge, even though most everyone willing to participate can put themselves in a better position, those who work more are more justly rewarded, which means the disparity between the most successful and those whose outcomes are more modest widens greatly. As the people who perceive themselves at the bottom look up, even though their floor has likely risen, they see how much further those ahead of them have risen and anger grows.

Such envy and resentment serve as the core of the Left and explains why their ideas can never truly be defeated or integrated away by any system. So long as the human instinct to want what another has remains, and people are willing to use these impulses to manipulate others, we will always deal with people who seek to gain through theft what they are either unable or unwilling to gain through merit. So, when we speak to them of fairness and opportunity, they might force a smile if they're tactful, but that's not what they want: They want to take your stuff, and then take you out for keeping from what they see as their birthright.

That's why identity politics emerged on the Left: not as a healthy celebration of culture and heritage to which all people of all races and ethnic groups should be equally welcome to participate, celebrating their own unique contributions, but as a means to organize entire groups in defense of their worst habits, to cultivate generational resentment, and ultimately supplement the existing malcontents with millions more. These people being brought in from foreign nations are not being introduced to America because of what they can contribute, but rather because they add chaos into our system, causing more strife and anger. And that's precisely why the Left fights so hard to maintain a system that disproportionately brings in random people from some of the most violent and regressive parts of the world. The rhetoric doesn't match the reality, but the way they keep us from speaking against what they are doing is to punish us with epithets like "racist," because they know that if they don't control us through fear and intimidation, we will destroy them with truth.

They've been in power a long time and we don't know, as of this moment, how much of their corruption Trump can and will be able to undo. Almost all of the items in the America First agenda are good policies we can build upon that represent first steps toward our restoration. Negotiating trade deals that put American workers on the same level as international business is important. Rebuilding the manufacturing base and upgrading core infrastructure within our nation is a national security issue. Removing the power of petty bureaucrats is welcome.

But we need more. We need a FBI, CIA, and IRS that aren't just waiting to be political weapons for the next Democrat in office. It's funny how every Tea Party organization was scrutinized by the IRS, but we can't even get the FBI to look in earnest at the tens of thousands of e-mails from the Clinton Foundation. The hypocrisy is blatant, and the favoritism toward the Left shows how deeply their corruption runs, and the daily struggle between our elected government and our unelected government is incredibly frustrating to the American people.

We need the wall. We need to end random visa lotteries. We need to go so much further in immigration than even the modest measures Trump is proposing, yet we see nothing happening because the institutional resistance to putting America First, though led by the Democrats, is bolstered by those Republicans who lack the courage to face the cultural consequences of stating that Americans might have a certain look, a certain set of values, or a certain set of ideals. Between the fear of being labeled by one of the hate groups like the SPLC or ADL who pass those judgments against others, and the donors who grease the skids for the bad old days to continue as long as they can, we see far too much corruption in the GOP which makes governing by the traditional and respectable way nearly impossible.

These struggles between the populist/nationalist effort that ultimately sustains Trump and the corporatist/globalist status quo will be a battle for the soul of the Right for the next few years. We know the latter faction is going to get what they can from Trump, take the edges off any reform that threatens their status or wealth, and in their own selfishness, refuse to look at the deeper issues like culture, immigration, integration, and identity that are the heart of the Left's attack. They will take the money, declare victory, and praise Trump, all the while missing what this movement must be about for this to be anything other than America's last hurrah.

We must help Trump do all that he can, to continue revealing the Left in all their vice, but also plan for the days after his administration is over. While no one can replicate his personality and presence, we can build upon the ideas we need in order to have a Republican Party which is excised of those who only use it for their own ends, and instead create a Republican Party that is led by those who have a genuine appreciation for nationalism, starting with our symbols, but understanding we must build our culture anew. I think we know something seriously went wrong from about 1965 forward, and we can undo what has been done if we're honest that we are in a cultural civil war.

If we act intelligently and forcefully in developing the Republican Party and using government to undo the power centers of those who oppose us, there is a narrow path whereby we might avoid our differences in opinion leading to hot conflict. If you find that statement too strong or alarmist, put this book down and go read **The Coming Civil War** first so you can see the four major ways and innumerable minor ways we've been set as a people against ourselves. Unless and until we fix that, America can only endure as either a legal despotism or an empire waiting to collapse when adversity overwhelms the spoils.

I know that's hard to hear, but I also know that I now have a reputation for saying the hard things and giving it to you straight. On some level, I believe our President knows these same things, but he's trying to inspire people out of them. God willing, that proves sufficient, in which case I would be happy to look like someone who was unduly paranoid. But history is against this effort proving anything more than just the opening, which is more than we might have expected, and still should be understood as the welcome opportunity to undo what was bad, reverse what is harmful, and build a new culture based upon the best parts of the old and some features that will inevitably be new that are all our own.

Having seen many Trump rallies, and with profound appreciation for his personal contribution, I'll call upon his direction here as we think about what we do after Trump. We don't give up, we fight on, and we remember what he said: that his movement to make America First and Make America Great is ultimately about us. We will have to do tough things, and we will have to call out that which we cannot abide, but if we work together and refuse to be constrained by those who hate us, therein lies our best chance to fix this and to return the investment Donald Trump made in America by creating a future that is brighter than ever before.

Chapter 2: The GOP Must Be More Than Economics

In this moment when things are going unusually well for the Right generally and Republicans specifically, it's worth taking a step back and looking at how we went from a culture and society that largely reflected our principles to one where their very reality is held in doubt by large segments of the population. Although the core American ideals and values themselves retain merit, the varying and sometimes overlapping definitions of those ideals, and the tepidness of Republicans about engaging on these terms, have proven inadequate to muster the mass appeal needed to protect our culture, and by extension, our national integrity.

The three arguments I remember hearing most frequently throughout my life are that the GOP is fiscally responsible, represents the moral majority, and wants smaller government. While compelling arguments exist in support of each of these positions, which I generally agree with, digging deeper into each version of the party shows how each idea creates certain vulnerabilities which have been ruthlessly exploited. They also have brought certain elements into the party who, by means of resources or influence have been able to exercise undue control to the point of proving either counter-effective or subverting the intent of a sound principle into deceptive policy.

Let's start with the easiest example which is that the Republicans are the party for rich people. The Left has used this canard for as long as they have existed, and it plays to their greatest rhetorical strength which is to present equality as a counterpoint to any other system. By doing so, their ideological view reaches the largest potential target audience, and that's why they take on a certain universal belief in their ideas which reminds one more of religion than reason. It becomes a tenet of faith to them to proselytize this idealized solution. Even though their rhetoric considers a lofty tomorrow where all benefit, they keep getting stuck with the reality that the only way we can approach true equality in our mortal coils is through bringing down the top to meet the bottom.

To be fair, when we have a society in which the top is in the stratosphere and has billions of dollars for owning some business or, less nobly, inheriting some fortune, and a working family cannot even afford to pay their bills as inflation outpaces income, such appeals will be more persuasive. I'm not one to indulge the politics of resentment, but Republicans need to understand how Democrats use these conditions so compellingly if we are to forge stronger networks to resist their barbs.

Now, the traditional Republican response, which is moral and fair, is to speak in terms of opportunity, conceding inequality as the logical outcome of different talents unequally applied and the result of foresight and effort to accomplish a goal. Such logic is incredibly sound as people deserve to realize their potential based upon their effort, but the problem starts when the Republicans, seeking to avoid all other issues, simply become a party where they strictly support what makes the most money for the most people.

The best feature about markets is they, at least between parties of similar sizes where one does not simply dominate another, as happens with monopolies, are voluntary exchanges where individuals or organizations get to price the value of their offerings in trade. For most values, it makes perfect sense to allow people to decide what they will offer and what they will pay with minimal interference. The problem is that what is usually true should not always be true, and market-based approaches fail in dealing with questions of human interest, when our most fundamental beliefs are put to the test.

At some point, the Republican Party adopted the radically libertarian position of being absolutely for free trade and assessing value whenever possible in a strictly market driven, detached, financial approach. I've often thought one reason the Right likes this method is because it allows for quantitative analysis as what appears, on the surface at least, as a fair way to compare apples to oranges by creating new categories that cover all fruit. We see this trend not just in politics, but across many professional fields where the rise of metrics and statistics has gone everywhere. But does it ever strike you that this is only window trapping to cover what a common-sense assertion might have done just a few years ago?

I'll give you a simple but profound example: How much is a human life worth? If you started to quantify your answer, you're doing it wrong. Because if humans merely have value as market actors, then we are really just property. And property, as we all know, can be bought, sold, and owned. A business owner functionally exerts a sort of ownership over a person, and while it may begin with a contract, has anyone else observed how the people on the lower end of those arrangements are increasingly made to give up more of their free will, not just during the agreed upon tasks, but upon their very presentation of themselves as free citizens outside of work?

You probably hate how the Left enforces compliance with their politically correct censorship regime, but is it any different than how corporate human resources departments now presume that you must subordinate your entire social being to the economic activity of your job, which you've volunteered to take, but which you functionally, unless you agree to be a ward of the state or are one of the few people able to fight your way out of the wage trap, are stuck upholding? I understand the need for common courtesy in the workplace, but we passed that long ago, and we've reached a point where our economics literally constrains our social expression. Perversely, this trend most hurts the most productive people, who find themselves least able to speak because they have the most to lose and therefore are the most monitored.

There was a time when we would have answered the question of the value of a human life in much different and moral terms, talking about the spirit of man, his potential, and his essential qualities. Such a reply would be far more uplifting than a quantitative analysis of lifetime earnings potential based upon education, location, class, and other variables, but we don't do that in our country or our party because we don't like having qualitative fights.

The Right likes talking in market terms because it anesthetizes us to the Left's cunning and dangerous assaults on language, class, and identity. Numbers can't be racist. Logic can't be racist. And yet, when we talk over them and they talk past us, we end up where we are now. The Right uses this language of merit, willfully oblivious to the fact that vast segments of the population have become blithely indifferent to the very concepts which are the logic upon which most of us build our lives. Conversely, the Left uses the language of acquisition, talking about life in terms of power structures and inequities, radicalizing their own supporters in two clever ways. Firstly, they take our success and use that as motivation to feed resentment. Secondly, they use emotional blackmail to persuade us to surrender ever growing shares of our own earnings to subsidize their growing and angry mob. And we submit, because we see it as a distraction from our individual and group efforts to realize success through the wealth which grants us stuff.

America's problem isn't our wealth. Objectively speaking, there has never been a wealthier country in history, which was true both during the poor economic policies of the Obama regime and under the more inspired leadership of Trump. But my point is that wealth will not bridge the social divide. In fact, it will likely only exacerbate the cultural gulf between the antagonists, which fits the reality we see happening in real time. So, when we see our President get up there and talk about the best unemployment numbers America has experienced in nearly a century, it sounds like success to us, but it sounds like an insult to the Left.

Fundamentally, the Left does not care about economics any more than is required to credibly hold their coalition of discontent together. Whereas those on the Right, more often than not, accept the general premise that the acquisition of goods to enjoy greater comfort and prosperity is the fairest way to enjoy a social life while allowing cultural differences to co-exist, the Left just sees this as us setting up society as the protector of a gifted status. Our success is an insult that plays perfectly into the resentment they coach, based upon their most sacred lie, which is that all men are equal. No men are equal, which is why we have different results, but their appeal to a form of fairness that is so universal that we all psychologically crave to be no man's lesser makes economics, the oft challenging effort to distribute inequality in fair proportions, seem hateful.

You can see how their cultural thinking reveals this in subtle and not so subtle ways. When you see someone driving a beater along the road with a thousand bumper stickers, have you noticed how that person almost always leans Left? They don't have the comforts we do, but what they have is faith, and it saddens me to say that institutionally speaking, even if many of us possess a private faith, we lack the courage or strength to put our fervor to contest against theirs in the public sphere. We retreat into the safer realms of economics and concede the cultural space, so while we get rich, we send our children to schools where they learn to hate the wealthy. Worse still, we pay for that privilege, empowering our own destruction because we keep thinking economics matters more than culture when there is scant historical evidence for that being true over the longer term.

Civilizations are defined by the very values they hold most dear and upon which they require adherence from all members. Markets exist as the opposite of this principle, a valuable component of any society whereby goods and exchange improve life through options, but which are ultimately corollary to who we are. If we are just a nation of traders, which some legitimately think, then all we are is the suit we wear when we awaken to offer everything for sale, even ourselves. Doesn't that seem somewhat hollow to you? I refuse to believe most people are like that, but that's all economic man can offer. Good economic policy helps improve life, but it cannot make us, should not define us, and will not protect us from people who play by other rules.

We can play by other rules as well without abandoning reason, but it is hard to get the Republican Party or organizational Right to move this way because it would conflict with our other values of restraint in the usage of government, which we'll cover in much more depth later. Perhaps more importantly, playing by other rules would conflict with the desires of those who fund the existing GOP.

Donors own both parties. Start with this understanding, which might be most easily reconciled if you consider that a corporation that does millions in business will gladly write off the expense of contributing to every side which might potentially help them. Paying thousands to have a say on how billions of other people's money is spent is sound financial thinking for any would be donor, although the long-term consequences of treating Washington as an auction house must inherently prove catastrophic over time as we now observe.

People ask how the Deep State came to power. They were the auctioneers who managed the vast military industrial complex arranging and maneuvering through wars and lesser conflicts that drove industries that made millions for contractors and many jobs for regular Americans as well. They created the revolving door between Congress and the lobbyists, made sure the streets were lined with cash, and realized the vision of America as a market, mercenary to the world, able to brand freedom onto any conflict, and to ensure the appropriations continued to roll.

Our Founders would be aghast at the size and scope of our government, our permanent bureaucracy, and how we ignored the Tenth Amendment and the entire spirit of the Constitution. I have zero doubt of this, as we have instead embarked on making a global empire of institutions and wealth, where banks run the show, print trillions of dollars and lend to one another in a world beyond consequence and conception, and where our lives in so many big and little ways exist only at their behest.

I don't have to agree with the Left's toxic crusade seeking equality to appreciate their critiques that the institutions of high finance, both in the public sector and the private sector do not serve the people. Most Republicans understood this perfectly fine during that odious bailout a decade prior, and we watched how the same people who still can't find money for a border wall, stole billions in taxpayer money, subsidizing the interest these banks and lenders charged the rest of us to repay their foolish investments while the regular folks were handed the bill if they could afford it, and left to rot if they could not. Our government is owned by the wealthy, not the people, and this first division which the Left created by encouraging the size of government to grow, was the root from which all these other schisms including the far more dangerous cultural split were able to find fertile ground.

While I think most conservatives and the rank and file of the GOP recognize their party is bought, or at least that an unsettling number of the leaders such as the late Senator McCain were, I'm not so sure they realize that this is a logical outgrowth of their retreat into being the party of the calculator and the balance sheet.

Do they realize the reason we now sit at the verge of being outnumbered, and why California was ultimately lost, is because bean counters figured out bringing illegal Mexicans across to pick fruit was a better bargain than paying a few extra dollars to have an actual citizen take upon the labor? They congratulated themselves again and again, from the 1980's onward for all the money they saved by bringing in outsiders, sending work to foreigners, and stripping the future assets of this country for resources today. But while we took the money, just like any other bad loan or transaction, the cost always comes due.

Now, although Trump is working feverishly to change this, we cannot produce all the goods we need to survive, our manufacturing sector had been decimated with people forced into service sector employment. Tens of millions of people from foreign cultures have been imported to drive down wages, hurting all Americans but helping a narrow segment of business, who never account for the social costs of welfare and integration as they are on the public balance sheet. Illegal immigrants now treat their presence here as a right, which makes sense considering the Right joined the Left for the last thirty years in saying "Hola Amigos," even as these people voted overwhelmingly for the Left. This is just one of the many costs we're now stuck paying because we were penny wise, but pound foolish.

Such is the consequence when the Republicans are strictly the party of free markets and economically sound principles. Two good ideas taken to their extreme become suicidal. We should generally favor markets and choice, especially as the Left reveals their totalitarian nature. We should look for policies where opportunity is rewarded, but we also cannot forget that opportunity needs to accrue to all Americans, and that the value of work is also in the dignity of meaning to those laboring.

We also need to stop thinking that everything can be traded, because we're better than that: We can stand on principle just as well as those we oppose, although this will force us to be willing to do two things we've generally hated: We will need to assert that our principles are not only better, but so much better that we will fight to see them realized in the public sphere, which under the current circumstances is going to mean government intervention, and that probably means for at least some time bigger government and more involved government.

One doesn't have to love those assertions to see the reason why a person like myself, once a conservative with libertarian leanings has become a reactionary. The Left will use government in every way possible to realize their goals, and they have spent fifty years siphoning funds through policy and subsidy to destroy our civil society and replace it with their own, with the universities, schools, and media leading the charge to force equality down our throats, and we simply have no other tools left with which to resist ... other than force.

Using the force of the state is the gentler of the two ways to offer meaningful opposition. The uglier way will be if we have to arm ourselves in resistance against an ideology that suggests the majority of those of us who make up the Right are guilty of the original sin of being born into a privileged group, and if you've studied any of the various European revolutions, ask how the Jacobins treated the French Aristocracy or ask the Romanovs how the Bolsheviks settled the score with their innocent children. Or, look at South Africa today if you have the stomach for it.

Understand that all the wealth in the world is not going to fix what is wrong in this country. At best, it might allow a few to buy their way out of the worst of the struggle. But while we make money now, they still poison the minds of our own children against us, they still use the media to defame us, and increasingly, they are turning the Internet into an echo chamber to isolate the very ideas that might offer resistance against their intended agenda.

The old Republican Party that is waiting in the wings to re-emerge post-Trump and get back to business cannot stop them. The ineffective party which campaigned on tax cuts, stripping people of their social security, and for free trade with more immigrants coming here as cheap labor, not only cannot stop them but will also never be able to win a national election again. They can pay for a few Senators and the Left would gladly deal with that version of Republicanism, because they know they can beat us if we become that every day of the week.

I'd rather not make things easy for them. Don't you agree?

Chapter 3: The GOP Must Fight the Culture War with Equal Force

Contrary to popular belief, Republicans usually win elections fought over culture. As much as the same political experts who still completely fail to understand Trump and nationalism will decry such division, people think in bright colors and appreciate when contrasts are drawn which allow them to make intelligent decisions. The Right, at its best, represents a vision of creation, continuity, and preservation of both new ideas and time-honored traditions. We represent innovation in how we are willing to push boundaries and explore our natural limits, and we also embrace the heritage of our people, celebrating the achievements of those who came before us as essential to our identity today.

What does the Left promise? They offer an orgy of destruction and nihilism where they push this idea of constant revolution to unmake those things people cherish and set us apart from one another by dividing us into a hundred different little tribes, so we beg for them, in their supposed wisdom, to serve as Hobbes' Leviathan above us. If you don't believe me, watch one of their rallies where you have women fetishizing themselves as their own genitals, or you see hooded black figures with smoke bombs, billy clubs, and those ubiquitous red flags waved menacingly as warning against what will happen should we dare to question them.

Do such figures represent the extreme Left when it comes to culture? Of course, but the difference between them and your average committed Democrat is only one of scale and timing, not one of intent. We face a culture that is so self-hating that it will seek to destroy America as we know it. They cannot do otherwise, because they know that our history, which is one of overcoming strife to realize success, is an existential threat to their narrative, and so we see the vigor with which they first rewrite and then erase our history altogether.

Let's take the second Unite the Right rally in Charlottesville as the perfect fulcrum for this conflict, because I happen to know more than a few of the principal figures involved. This event shows the raw reality of how this culture war proceeds in real time in the absence of political posturing. Following the letter and spirit of the law, Jason Kessler arranged to have a rally whose stated purpose was to "Unite the Right" and whose organizational purpose was to protest the removal of Confederate monuments from Charlottesville, Virginia, a town whose very history is steeped in that conflict.

They worked meticulously according to the letter of the law, working with police and the civil government to ensure a safe and peaceful rally. A plan had been agreed to by all parties to prevent the protesters from coming into any conflict with the radical Leftists who were spending their parents' money to become indoctrinated to hate this country.

So, what happened? On the day of the rally, the city government, which leans heavily Democrat, ignored its own established plans and instead of keeping the sides separated, funneled those men speaking against the erasure of monuments dedicated to a seminal period in American history into a gauntlet of violent and armed Leftists. No one ever mentions that these Leftist hoodlums had no permit to gather, because as you'll note the rule of law doesn't apply to the Left because they have social justice on their side, a magical sanction for whatever illegal acts they commit. And just as you'll note with sanctuary cities, they feel free to ignore the laws which don't suit their tastes, allowing criminals to go free while they persecute patriots.

Did you know that the Unite the Right activists out there were attacked? There were weapons, pepper spray, and I even know of a person attacked by an improvised flame thrower. Following directions from city hall, the police looked the other way, and they created this chaos so their friends in the media could tell their false narrative.

The media tells how Nazis were rising in Virginia, and then proceed to gather documentation on the face of every man brave enough to walk publicly against the erasure of our history. Ironically, they were able to identify (and inform the employers of) every person wearing American regalia or sporting Dixie colors, but they just somehow never managed to figure out who the person was who was wearing a swastika. Does it ever make you wonder who really put that person there and who they represented? Maybe it's just a bit too convenient, because it creates the narrative once more that those defending our culture – American culture – are just racists who need to be stamped out.

It would have been just that, another set of lies, save for the death of Heather Heyer. Check out the videos yourself and see that a man who was in the vicinity, who may or may not have had anything to do with the events, found his car surrounded by a beat mob angrily gesticulating and breaking things with weapons. He did an entirely rational thing, trying to escape the angry crowd surrounding him, and yet the narrative presented is that he was the assailant in trying to protect his person against an unauthorized and clearly belligerent group of unknown people.

To his credit, President Trump saw this reality, which is why he didn't rush to condemn these activists. To their detriment and shame, nearly every other Republican virtue signaled to the tune of the media drum, which repeats the lies that Whites are bad, minorities are good, our historical culture is evil, and progressives are virtuous. Our idiot politicians forsook the very men and women most willing to fight to preserve what they claim to support, again and again, and we wonder why we end up with an antiseptic Republican Party that doesn't know how to fight for its culture.

I never punch right. I don't agree with everyone to my right, and I'm far enough out there to deal with some extreme figures. But you'll note that you never see Democrats attacking socialists or communists – instead they work together on the many issues where they agree to amplify their message by linking the ground troops of their more fanatical believers with the more moderate positions that policy leaders and the majority of their supporters inherently take. We don't do this on the Right, because we instead like to signal to one another about how our individual views are the most correct, reckoning it virtue to refuse cooperation in pursuit of some perfect idealism.

Functionally, what that has accomplished is that the intersectional Left now controls the dominant cultural narrative in America, and we've so internalized defeat that until relatively recently, we had experienced only decades of moral victories, and cultural failures, by falling on our swords on issue after issue. Marriage is no longer between a man and woman. Hell, a man and a woman aren't even the only sexes any more if you believe what the Left offers as cultural reality. It seems insane that we never stood up to call these ideas lunacy, but we can't because we've been so busy comforting ourselves with the consolation of being right and standing against those who might agree with us because they disagree on other things, that we've done nothing but enable our enemies to have free rein.

I use the word enemy in full knowledge of its strength. While there are certainly many misguided people among the Left who are just following along the social narrative, do not delude yourself into believing they do not know what they are doing. They know precisely how to foster division, how to attack what is healthy, and to use rhetoric and relativism to destroy the foundations of the society and the nation to allow them access to unfettered control of the state. If you don't understand how all this works, there are many excellent works covering the Frankfurt School where these hateful ideas were pioneered and familiarizing yourself with how the Left truly operates will be time well spent.

Here, my goal is not to cover what they do, but to talk about how we must come together to resist them. Although we might differ on the intensity of our ideas and certain details, the Right actually is inherently far more united than the Left because our core idea is that quality trumps quantity. We believe in the search for fairness and equity while also dealing with the reality that nature and our Creator gave us unequal but still distinctive and valuable endowments. We are all builders; they are all destroyers.

It's hard to build a building with two designers and I couldn't imagine writing a book like this with another author, which is why we struggle to articulate and defend our culture against the mob of the left. They use numbers to overwhelm us, and even though we might have better ideas, we end up isolated and divided. So, what I propose in order to overcome this, is that we work to support our creators, where writers share each other's books, and the faithful congregate together, and the moral speak up for sanity against at least those ideas the vast majority of Americans can clearly recognize as not wanted.

We can win those battles, like standing against transgenderism as a mental sickness, instead of indulging the delusional fantasies of the Left. Moreover, in so doing, we reveal we care more than they do about our fellow people, which we should as nationalists, rather than strengthening their charade that the culture of diversity and tolerance is virtuous.

Diversity just means an unwillingness to seek distinctions, and tolerance is the nice way of saying: "I care so little about what you do that I will allow you to do anything so long as you leave me alone." We have made that bargain for years, hoping a little tolerance would bring peace and quiet from their tumult, and what have we seen? Can we ever concede enough to satisfy these lobbies who start out just asking for acceptance and end up now dragging us into legal warfare for our legitimate expression of disagreement with their fabricated agendas? It's utterly insane we've let our country to come to such a point, but this is what happens when you categorically refuse to pass judgment on any ideas.

We live in the realm of fantasy now, where the Left believes reality is a morality play replicating Harry Potter and every God-fearing Republican is a Death Eater in waiting. I wish I were making that up, but they have become so unhinged because their culture has no connection to reality, because reality itself is a threat to their vision, so it must be unmade. History must be rewritten. Tradition must be discarded. People who dissent must be replaced – outvoted if possible but ostracized if not.

Such a scheme would be laughable if not for the fact it actually seems to be working. We play by their rules, restraining ourselves from speaking up for things we know to be inherent to the human condition, hiding our virtue, and refusing to comment upon the vices we see in anything other than whispered tones. We restrain ourselves based upon our own inherent decency, and the uncertainty all men feel in making moral judgments. And yet, even though we may never perfectly know truth, does it not seem that we at least have sufficient discernment to know wickedness when it is directly in front of us?

I do not fear to label the Left as evil, because they seek through their culture to take what is beautiful, spiritual, and distinctive within each of us and reduce it to that which is basic, material, and animal. They explicitly shun aspiration and achievement, believing these values rest only on prejudice as they deny the ability to use reason to differentiate the value of one judgment against another. As all people must be equal, so too must all ideas be held equal, and the only metric by which they may be judged is the degree of infringement a set of beliefs places upon another person's perception of reality. Such a framework can only hate success, reality, and health, because whenever people are drawn to any morality which exists independent of their own obsession with toxic equality, they will declare its instructions hateful and seek to destroy that morality and all who follow it.

In America, they have largely accomplished this goal. Through a combination of social pressures and economic disincentives, they have either co-opted or destroyed far too many of the existing churches and other civic institutions to such a degree that they now offer only token opposition to these ideas. They made speaking about policy a crime by putting donations to the church at peril and then used government to enforce silence. Then they had other levels of government or external friends replace the money given by parishioners with government funds for approved purposes. Where Christians once worked exclusively for the benefit of their community, how many institutions now serve Leftist causes to sustain themselves in the guise of serving our culture?

Living in New England, where the collapse into secularism is nearly complete, it's stunning how effectively the Left was able to employ access to government funds and a series of overlapping legal regulations to essentially transform the entire culture of a group who was only tangential to the government. They knew what they were doing, and in their faith that their gospel of equality was correct, they showed no restraint in using every tool government could offer them to realize their vision.

The cautious will note, rightly I believe, such passion absent reason can only lead to tragic outcomes. History agrees with this analysis as the cultural Left has proven both incredibly adroit at gaining power, and incredibly inept about using it once attained. However, knowing these things, and knowing that simply offering the option to do nothing as an alternative is what we are presently suggesting, do we want to allow the Left to leverage their cultural hegemony into a position where we must live those sad generations of squalor and despair to be reborn into a saner way of living?

I think we can do much better. Let's pick these cultural fights, not because we seek to micromanage how people live in accordance with our particular beliefs, but because we should no longer be bullied through their intimidation into allowing the Left to define normalcy. Agreeing to a degree of tolerance was perfectly reasonable, but this idea that we must offer special sanction to every protected group they can imagine must stop immediately. We cannot allow them to endlessly divide us into smaller and smaller groups based upon divergent identity and belief. We need commonalities also, and not just those of economic reality or legal status, but core beliefs that we share as a nation which unite us.

We need to be a moral people. We need to have the family once more at the center of both our public and private life, and to bridge the cultural gap between men and women. We need to reclaim the values upon which America was built and was founded: Values of industry, integrity, and intelligence, built upon our White Western Christian heritage, and assert those values as the irreducible beliefs upon which we will guide our ship. To assert such is not the same as requiring formal adherence to every specific belief, but rather to reset the mainstream to something healthy that we can share, and to recognize people's value in their ability to work within such framework.

The Left has worked tirelessly since 1965 to destroy this unity, both through cultural dissolution and through introducing immigrants not meant to be assimilated, but rather to serve to destroy the existing order by bringing foreign ideas in such numbers as to create strife at the center of America. They have succeeded. Multiculturalism is real, and it is killing America. If it is not reversed, we will either balkanize into multiple nations, collapse into no nation at all, or exist only under totalitarian despotism. America can only exist as it was as one united culture, and if we are not willing to fight using every tool at our disposal to realize that, America will fall.

The good news is that as dire as those predictions seem, we remain the silent majority and the moral majority. Most people agree with these positions, but they do not speak out for fear of persecution. For years, we have been silent accomplices to such action, but a time of choosing is upon us where we can choose a different path. We can stop shunning the righteous and indulging the profligate. We can speak up for our values and govern unapologetically according to those values. We can even, if we are so bold, use government to restrain the culture of death they push in our schools and in our media.

As always, it is a question of will. They have the will to power to push through their egalitarian utopia against any opposition. Do we have the same energy and resolve with which to not just oppose them, but to offer a more compelling alternative which decisively exposes their lies and allows us to realize a more perfect union? Our ancestors who braved uncertain seas and much danger to get here had enough faith. Our Founders who fought a revolution and their progeny who fought a Civil War to more clearly define who we were had enough faith. Do we have enough faith in ourselves to take this back?

If the resolve is there, the policies are not so complicated. This America might be a little different, scarred by our close encounter with the radicals of the Left who are so close to seizing power and dominion over us. In order to secure the future, we may need to assume certain authority with which we are not so comfortable, yet for the dangers we face now, we might yet find greater security for these next few generations in having met the threat of our time and having overcome their deceit.

Chapter 4: Smaller Government Isn't Always Better.

Republicans and conservatives alike take pride in the assertion that they support smaller government. The idea that people should make decisions for themselves is a natural extension of the liberties enshrined clearly in our Constitution. And these liberties reflect, in themselves, an understanding of natural law. In healthier times, it would probably make for an intelligent bedrock principle upon which we could base all our other political activities, but as we live in uncertain times, we need to more carefully examine this contention.

The basis upon which the Right fundamentally opposes large government is twofold. The first principle as listed above is our belief that people make better decisions for themselves, or less generously, have the right to make decisions for themselves where the government has no legitimate interest in preventing such expression. The second factor is that power does tend to corrupt, or more precisely, serves as invitation for the corruptible to misuse. For these reasons, the default position on the Right has long been to oppose government intervention into public life because a power granted quickly becomes a power misused.

I understand why the conflict between Left and Right was fought on this basis, and for many years, it made perfect sense. If Franklin Roosevelt had not come to power and created the sorts of social programs like Social Security and the permanent military state which never demobilized after the Second World War, how different would our government be, and how many fewer ways would government have been able to intervene in our lives compared to today? A government lacking such funding and authority would have proven far less capable at degrading our culture through this process of shifting authority from civil society to the state, and we were right to fight for smaller government in that era.

Yet, for as true as it remains that government tends to assert greater authority over our lives every time it grows and the very real risk of corruption that invites, it remains equally true that absent a collapse, government is very rarely reduced in size after taking on new responsibilities. Once people become acclimated to the idea that government should be involved in an area, not only do people begin to expect the government to manage the problem, but we also see private actors formerly involved in these areas fade away such that, absent doing nothing, there ceases to be a private alternative in many cases to state management on these issues.

There are obviously workarounds, and the example of the state funding private entities in a competitive context is an excellent model in certain areas that represents a Right-thinking solution to a problem caused by Leftist overreach which cannot simply be undone. The key point, however, is that once people expect the state to handle an issue, the power rarely reverts back to the people themselves, and the Right's unwillingness to offer their own solutions to these developing areas of policy has been a severe strategic failure. This represents yet another area the Left opened for public discourse, and where, by their refusal to play, the Right has surrendered the field.

Health care and pensions alone make up much of the non-discretionary funding within the Federal budget, encompassing well over half the spending of our government. Yet, for decades we have offered no serious solutions to address either issue as we simply asserted that the government shouldn't be involved in these areas. From a strictly Constitutional perspective, this is undoubtedly true. But from the perspective of popular sovereignty, which is to say the government which governs best should be responsible to the publicly expressed desires of the people, it is far less certain.

Here, Trump's instincts are helpful. Although it was seen as anathema at the beginning of his campaign in 2016, he was careful to intentionally distinguish himself from all other Republicans who rushed to speak of free markets and smaller government by ensuring to the people that their pensions, which were earned by paying into a system, no matter how poorly it was designed and how it had been misappropriated would remain intact. He likewise committed to ensuring that the least well among us would not be discarded for having pre-existing conditions in any future health care reform. He put people above ideas – which is the very essence of nationalism, the core of his belief, and the alternative against which we should measure the efficacy of small government, both in terms of political appeal and in the ability to satisfy the demands of the people.

It is important to understand that these issues take on life or death relevance for people who would otherwise agree with much more of what the Right believes, but who are forced to sometimes vote otherwise to protect the means of their survival. Understanding this, Trump narrowed that gap while still remaining open to smarter government driven solutions, inclusive of private innovation and choice, but guaranteeing that if a better private solution failed, an imperfect public solution would be sustained. I guarantee you that turned some votes in Pennsylvania, Wisconsin, and Michigan, and just might have been the secret that flipped the entire American electoral map.

As much wisdom as we can take from the Founders and what they set out in the Constitution, we should not forget the world we live in today is radically different than the largely agrarian rural existence of 18th Century America where over 90% of the population were self-sufficient farmers. Urbanization, industrialization, and now information is changing our society, pushing people into contact with one another in more ways and more often than ever before, and it would be naïve to think as this happens, that people wouldn't naturally seek new rules to govern how these interactions are managed.

A Constitutionalist might note this to be true, but argue these issues are best left to be governed at the local level or by the individual states, which depending upon the particular issue might make better sense. But we now must reserve for ourselves the right to determine how and at what level to deal with novel issues, recognizing there are times and places, because of the import of what is involved, and how important some matters are, both to all Americans and our continuing unity as a people, that Federal authority might be the best path forward.

To offer the least controversial example I can consider, look at the Department of Defense. As someone whose tastes tend strongly toward isolation for many reasons, it pains me to admit this, but having a strong standing Army and Navy serve as a deterrent which, used properly, would prevent more conflict than it would cause. The Constitution only calls for the commission of the Navy but does not consider the need for a permanent standing Army, not to mention the various industries which exist around maintaining and expanding this capacity. Yet, I think few Americans would gladly contemplate giving up these weapons, because we understand we live in an uncertain world where there are people who have certain ideas we would not wish to see imposed upon us.

We would likely differ greatly about how and when to use the capacities both in defense and in proactive action to protect against future threats, and reasonable people will likely assert there have been times when these capacities have been misused. Yet, in spite of these many mistakes, does anyone feel less safe for having a powerful military, even though it takes much money and expands the Federal sway considerably?

As stated, the reason we support a strong military is because it offers defense of our nation, a word that has many different meanings which we speak openly but perhaps consider too lightly. A nation is a group of people who define themselves as sharing some common attribute. In the case of the military, the definition is largely legal and geographic, but not entirely as their recruitment calls upon certain martial virtues like valor and sacrifice, and we see that the people who voluntarily commit to our mutual defense often emerge from those areas where the traditional American culture has not been subsumed. Nations always have ideas at the heart of their existence, and to defend a nation means both to understand what a nation is about, and to work to preserve that idea.

The question this begs, which has no perfect answer but must be considered in the particulars of each circumstance is: How does our state best help preserve our nation? On the Right, the standard dogma for the last few decades is government should get out of our way, so our people can forge the nation we choose, but if we are honest, we can see that model has proven ineffective at constraining the Left from their countervailing vision. What we have essentially seen since Johnson is that when the Left takes power, government pushes the culture toward their egalitarian pose, and when the Right takes power, government takes a breather from the cultural battles. In short, we have been able to pause their progress, but we have neither stopped them nor shifted the movement in our own direction because we don't trust government.

Maybe we hold ourselves to too high a standard, and instead of needing to trust government to always do the right thing, we should admit we would accomplish more by trusting ourselves to use government more intelligently than our opponents. If we move beyond a purely economic view of government and root our actions in a clearly defined and accessible morality, I would trust Republicans with the exercise of significantly more power than they currently assume, and would gladly support them as a counterpoint to what I know the Left will – not might – do should they inherit such authority. We have seen, as with our brave military, that when motivated by clear purpose for the good of the entire nation, government can be effective.

This shift is at the heart of Trump's challenge to the existing status quo, where we move from a conservative free market party based on economic prosperity and social noninterference to a nationalist party where we consider carefully who our people are, defining the ideas and values that will unify us together in moral action, and assess each area of social and public discourse through a more pragmatic prism of what is good for our people and what is bad for our people.

For too long, we have let systems govern us where we subjugate our lives to the idea of which polarity is best. Is the market better than the state? Is tolerance better than discernment? Is less government better than more government? The questions themselves are perfectly reasonable and will always be at the crux of political thinking, but our misstep is in thinking methodology makes for some ideology that will solve all our problems. Every problem is different, so instead of fitting our challenges to a set method, we could instead as nationalists ask what problems most impact our people and seek out the best solution available, retaining our preferences toward liberty, responsibility, and morality, but recognizing that imperfect solutions to genuine needs are better than ignoring problems that fester into precisely the breeding ground of discontent upon which the Left flourishes.

Once we define who are our people are, which will be the major challenge ahead of us, and one from which we have run for far too long, it becomes incumbent upon the Right as the voice of both reason and quality to offer solutions to these problems. Most will come from the private sector. Some will not. We need to understand this as we walk into these conflicts, and most crucially, we must recognize that if we refuse to address the legitimate problems of our people, then we will lose their confidence and they will seek other solutions, no matter how absurd they may be, because at least the other side will show concern about what is bothering our people.

We come from the party of reason, as emissaries to the tribe of feelings. If you doubt me, check out the psychological research that proves we spend just a second or two deciding, and then the rest of our time building a rationale in defense of our initial instinct or feeling. People are overwhelmingly governed by their emotions, and if they think you don't care about them, which is what so many of our fellow citizens hear when we state that government shouldn't be involved with their problems, they will not merely ignore you, but will ultimately come to despise you. And while reality is such that we cannot be all things to all people and try to solve all problems, it's an entirely valid criticism to say the Republicans have for a very long time had little to say on major social and economic issues like health care as just one example that represents an existential crisis to millions of Americans.

I'll share a deeply personal example. My wife has chronic Lyme Disease, an epidemic that is essentially being swept under the rug here in the Northeast, but which is spreading nationally. The test which checks for its existence has a dismal assessment rate, the doctors who lead the national organization for speaking about Lyme have been demonstrated to overwhelmingly be on the take for pharmaceutical companies who offer treatments that don't work for the disease. So, they lobby the Centers for Disease Control (CDC) to reclassify the disease more narrowly to make their products appear more effective, and this corrupt bargain also classifies hundreds of thousands of suffering people outside diagnosable medical expertise so they receive no treatment at all. It's an awful and dehumanizing condition that impacts both the body and brain, and which insurance companies are only too glad to not cover because the cost of treatment is prohibitive with no clear cure in sight. If someone said they'd run this government in such a way that big pharmaceutical companies could no longer use the FDA as a clearing house, even if they were Left of center, someone even as radical as myself would give them serious consideration. And that's because not just my wife's quality of life, but her life itself, is at stake.

If you're a politician who tells me that isn't your problem, and the alternative says they will help, I can totally understand the person who tells you to go straight to hell and who will never listen to you again. The Republicans, through their adherence to the orthodoxy of what government can and cannot do, radicalized millions of Americans against them who see our party as nothing but heartless bastards talking about money and values they won't practice. So many of these people are ones we never should have lost, but we did because we put our ideology above the well-being of our nation, and the emergent Right needs to have a better answer. Even if we can't solve every problem, we can at least care enough to admit that problems this large are a responsibility we all share together, and to tackle them thoughtfully and humanely.

I have no doubt the arguments we will have on questions like this will be fierce and temperamental, with many hurt feelings. We will disagree, as we do best, because we are usually better educated and more thoughtful. We will get angry with one another and want to tell each other to go away. And yet, if we can endure through these tempests, do you doubt such discussion would make better policy for our people? Do you think the solutions we struggle to forge, earnestly if painfully, will be better than what the Left offers in their delusional belief of absolute equality and willful ignorance of economic reality? Most importantly, do you believe our people will appreciate the effort and reward us with their support, the reason for which we all devote so much time and energy into this sordid game?

Frankly, I think America is craving that sort of leadership, and I hope we have the courage in the Republican Party to stop being the party of smaller, and start being the party of better. We will make mistakes and should always be mindful of our limits and approach them with humility, but we should also recognize that sometimes the best we can do is pretty damned good, and much better than doing nothing at all. In this world of politics, sometimes we forget that in the end we're here to help our people. When we make things simpler like that, and adopt a core principle like that: Support our people – those who reside in our space and share our core values – I don't see how we can lose so long as we are willing to fight as hard for them as those who stand against us do to destroy what we have been given, what we have built, and all that we love.

The Left lives for the dialectic. Stop playing by their rules and we will start beating them quickly.

Chapter 5: Nationalism's Beginnings – Laws and Symbols

I don't pretend to keep aware of the latest academic discourse, largely because so much of it strikes me as the rationalization of preconceived fictions along Marxist or other similar intellectual paths, but my recollection of political science was that it was obsessed with state formation, how laws should be created, and how policy responds to popular desire. But what has always struck me and is incidentally the reason my major was in history and not political science, was that the nation part of the nation-state is deliberately mis-characterized and has not received the consideration it merits for entirely too long.

These terms are used somewhat interchangeably in common discourse, which sometimes makes sense as there is overlap in who they refer to, but the differences are just as important. A nation is a group of people who share a common identity. A state is the governing body of a clearly defined political body. Historically, our modern state emerged from the age of kings whose territory was held on a more personal basis, to serve at least theoretically as popularly sovereign governments whose job was to defend the interests of a particular people: The nation.

States exist throughout the world without nations, but in those cases where we see either divided nations or multiple nations trapped beneath a single political system, we often see greater strife than with states who service only a single nation or whose members all belong to that same single nation. More than any other factor, the greatest contributor to stability in any state, independent of compelling acceptance through force, is shared national identity.

Why should this matter so much? The shortest answer is because when things go wrong, the investment people have in one another determines their ability to overcome adversity, and crises are inevitable in the world, and the interaction between peoples. If you care about your neighbor and believe their welfare will directly impact your own, or at least that you have a stake in their well-being, you will be much more likely to deal with difficulties by offering aid versus closing up and taking a defensive posture.

The very premise of civilization is that we can accomplish more collectively, through specialization of labor, enabled by some degree of trust and standardization, and that we benefit more from working together versus working alone. What distinguishes both civilizations and nations from each other are the specific core principles around which this organization is undertaken, with Western Civilization being currently centered around the ideas of reason, limited government, individual autonomy, and personal responsibility.

All these values precede and transcend the state whose purpose is merely to ensure compliance with these values, and in an ideal scenario, serve as the body for the protection of these values against foreign intrusion and internal subversion. With varying degrees of success, the previous two centuries saw states take on these roles admirably, and to use our American example, enshrined and codified these beliefs within our beloved Constitution which clearly delineates the limited authority of government and the liberties reserved to the citizens.

Something changed recently. Beginning some time after World War II, and coming fully into the public eye following our victory in the Cold War, nations were deliberately disregarded by the policy makers at multiple levels and instead they have been trying to construct a superstate above their respective peoples, most often without their consent and often without their knowledge, to force at least large chunks of humanity into a single tribe and then nation. The European Union is probably the best example of this thinking whereby sovereign nations are now increasingly beholden to an undemocratic institution that mandates policies on law, borders, tariffs, and migration which many people do not want and to which states themselves are being held in subjugation by a combination of financial carrots and sticks, presaging the creation of an overstate to subsume the nations. This pilot model seems to be the preferred global path being charted for all the nations of at least the West, and certainly has the favor of the Left here in America as they repeat the global citizen mantra.

What is the price? Nations will be lost. The unity of a common people who share common bonds and who are motivated by care and concern gives way to states which only mandate and enforce their beliefs. It's a world where all police officers give way to serving as Orwellian law enforcement, where debate and discussion over policy from the people themselves must necessarily surrender to compliance and conformity. Safe spaces might be allowed, but dissent will not be tolerated. So now we see the inescapable totalitarianism seeking such equality between disparate beliefs and actors yawning upon that red horizon as clearly as it once did from the Soviets who imagined a blunter approach leading to this same outcome.

Most of us on the Right do not want to see our nation subsumed and understand that every time America commits to some foreign entanglement, we increase our risk of such an outcome. How many wars have we been drawn into due to the United Nations? Because of NATO? How many jobs have we lost to multinational trade agreements, and how many resources have we surrendered due to global compacts on any and every topic? Did the people have a say?

Worse still, as you will mostly be aware, as part of this plan to realize a single state for humanity, we see the forced homogenization of all peoples into uniform "nations." Please understand our elites see the migration of Latinos into America and Muslims into Europe as a desired outcome, using their comments about economic opportunity and diversity as subterfuge for their agenda whereby they hope to bring up the Third World by giving away what we in the civilized West have struggled for years to create. Their system requires a new equilibrium, and though they use the happy rhetoric of lifting people up, the reality is the new center will only be achieved by tearing our prosperous nations down. Therefore, you see the Left, who serves as the primary but not the only engine for these changes, pushing for open borders, welfarism, and using the rhetoric of prejudice to compel compliance from populations who both do not and should not want these changes.

The way we need to fight these plots is to embrace nationalism within our nation, and within each nation once more. We must assert our rights as sovereign citizens to have our elected governments represent solely our national interest, and work in concert with all other nations who share the same belief. We need to reveal ourselves as the true stewards of both popular consent and intellectual diversity, recognizing that distinctive cultures with different peoples and divergent ideas on truth are not simply interchangeable, and end this charade wherein we pretend taking people who see the world opposite from how we do leads to anything other than chaos and conflict. America for Americans needs to become the rallying cry, and we are on that path.

Who are Americans? That is the question we must answer, and it will be a hellacious struggle. If we define "American" to mean "anyone who wants to be here," we've already lost the argument to the globalists. We can define this by race, by culture, by belief, by ideas, by law, or some combination of such. But whatever choice we make, we need to define our American nation in a way that unifies a core of people behind a common set of principles and with the willingness to defend one another and govern in the best interests of all those so defined.

How does one begin this process? Some people argue that we need to remove all people who are unlike us, and while that policy would have clear benefits, it also runs against our most commonly held moral instincts, as most of us know people who are unlike us in some ways, but who share our core values and wish to contribute. The virtuous few who integrated into the old American way of industry and integrity, are now used as a shield and a pretext against moving against the larger number arriving who seem resistant to such assimilation, must be considered based upon virtue and value in consideration of who belongs. To exclude them would be immoral, to neglect them would give away too much, and to include them would denude the Left of their most useful means by which they have prevented the Right from action.

Considering all these possibilities, I argue for a three-step process that is a novel way of thinking about nationalism, where we work from our current position toward increasingly greater stability, more social, cultural and racial homogeneity, and clearly assert first on a legal and then increasingly on a cultural basis, the distinctiveness and exceptional uniqueness of America.

Inherently, the first step in this long process must be to control the laws and state by which our nation is to be reforged. Should the Left control the Federal government at any time, they unfailingly introduce foreign people and foreign authority into our system, subverting all efforts to preserve our national identity, attacking our common culture, and using existing identity and national affiliations external to the United States as a wedge to disable our ability to define ourselves on our own terms. They love this because they are internationalists, globalists, and egalitarians, who make it clear they see the only exceptional traits of America as being our hate, bigotry, and violence. This is evident in how they rush to erase our history. They show that they want a blank slate for both our country and all others, so they can tell their fantasy of universal human enlightenment, and heaven on Earth. You don't have to be a Christian like I am to see how this conceit oozes with false pride, and to understand the violence and dehumanization that would be required to try to force so many people into compliance with one another.

We have a better alternative, and we must begin with civic nationalism. To my friends who argue that we need a common culture to transcend the state, or who say we need a solid ethnic foundation to ensure our instincts are primed to support such nation building here at home, I agree. We will talk about those ideas and promote these as the development of a maturing nation which are inescapable and important steps, without whom full nationhood will never be achieved, but they are not the starting steps of this process. We must start by getting control over our own destiny, and that means the people who have a vision of America preserving itself must be writing the laws, defending the symbols, and articulating our shared values.

I honestly believe most nations and ethnicities formed a similar way. While it goes without saying that the connections of families in close proximity and of a common genetic lineage are the basis for ethnic development, those ethnicities which were successful were often motivated either around a single leader, or institutions whose ideas were so compelling they created a civilization or nation around them to realize their potential. Think of the origins of the West, in the Greek study of mathematics, rhetoric, and philosophy, or the Romans whose mastery of law, architecture, and engineering allowed them dominion over others. We are here, sitting upon the hill, watching our fellow citizens granting entrance to the barbarians at the gates while we search for those ideas whereby we might organize ourselves into first resistance and then dominance. In time, such ideas could become a culture unto themselves, able to assert their value in the world through success, and we need that outcome, but that's for another day.

Now, with the enemy at and within the gates, we need allies, we need courage, and we need the willingness to impose whatever laws are needed to prevent them from either giving away all we built and have had bestowed upon us, or to avoid them gaining control that will allow their hoodlums to pick us off one by one. I use these images as metaphor here, but to be perfectly blunt, we're not all that far from realizing such battles in hard reality, as the street battles between the far Left, who enjoys the support of their entire faction, and the few brave men on the far Right, who have stood for our civilization alone, presage what will come if we do not act soon and decisively.

So, we start where we can, and we build upon what Trump is doing. We wrap ourselves in the flag of America, the symbols of past success, the honored memory of what our ancestors sacrificed to create this opportunity, and in the demand for sound leadership that puts America first. Such first steps are always rhetorical, but if we push for the logical policy positions which follow in a nationalist plan of action, America would be much improved. We should end most immigration, demand far more from our citizens, stop subsidizing both the individual and institutional actors who speak against our heritage, and recognize that in order to preserve our liberties and rule of law, we will need to invest new authority in our government.

The last line might scare you. You might prefer cultural institutions to do freely what government does through compulsion. I would also, but the Left has killed so many of them, and owns most of the remaining cultural entities who enjoy dominance. The Left will show no restraint in imposing their politically correct orthodoxy on us, through force if necessary. You might want to build a culture to fight back, and we must do that, but we don't have the time to accomplish this organically because of how they have used in-migration as a weapon to destroy our unity and turn this democracy into a power grab for globalism. The voting patterns are unmistakable here – the rate at which new progressives are being brought in far outpaces the speed by which a restored culture can ferment.

Our choices end up being to either push for what we want or accept what they will give us. There was an earlier time where other avenues remained open, but it is the sad reality the Left has forced us along a certain path which they will, to some extent, dictate by how they motivate their own supporters. Identity politics, as one example, are here to stay. Even the best civic nationalism isn't going to awaken the majority of the minority population, because in the momentary perspective of who is willing to give the most for their support, the worst tendency of our current democracy, we cannot give them what the Left will offer them: Everything we possess.

These limitations are why so many people on the Right, who think deeply on these issues, have retreated as far as their situation allows, and why so many smart people think a collapse is the only way we advance forward. They believe there is no motivational path forward to restore America to functionality, given all the foreign attributes grafted onto us and given also how our culture is avowedly hostile to this project, but they miss one point: The raw exercise of power in support of the popular will, especially when buttressed by sound values and brave men, can overcome any effort which basically rests on the resentment and apathy of others.

Trump stands on the Rubicon but does not appear to want to cross it. I wish he would, because that would be the best option here, but if he doesn't, someone else must. We must all form ranks, as a united Right, in discussion and defense of clearly chosen ideas, open to all citizens who share these commonly expressed goals and we must be willing to use our government to sustain the vision we want and destroy the corruption which threatens us all.

I will tell you how I know this is the best path forward. There is nothing so frightening to our enemies as nationalism itself, the idea that people come together in voluntary bonds – not bondage based upon fear or envy – and take control of our lands while bringing people together by virtue. We can respect authority and liberty – just as we know how good parents who set boundaries create the space where their children can learn the right values. We can break through all these traps and lies they've set for us, when we define ourselves as people who are good, moral, just, and self-reliant, and when we refuse to allow them to guilt or shame us any more into giving power or control to their sick games. We can have all the heart in the world, but we need to stop being beaten into paying for them to take over our responsibilities as a common people.

We need strong leaders now and we need stronger laws. These will cause fights – whether they be social, political, or cultural. It's better we pick these now while the majority retains our beliefs versus later when the only option to stand for preservation of our values and quite possibly our very existence will be pitched battles. We need to stop sacrificing tomorrow for today, be clear and honest with our fellow Americans about these challenges before us, and to create a civic spirit of renewal, of martial valor, of virtue based upon our heritage and foundational beliefs, and of statesmen instead of politicians.

It starts when we pick up the flag and say to the Left, no more will we accept your definitions about us, and no longer will you have any power over us. It builds when we take the lies they state and say: "we declare right and wrong as separate and knowable, and recognize that what is ours is not yours!" We do not want your false equality and promises of squalor. We want to be free, to be difficult and different, and to achieve what we dream possible.

For years, they have prevented us from saying what must be said, the necessary precursor to organizing for what must be done. Trump, through his utter destruction of the politically correct culture that bound us, has created the opening. So, for all those who understand our common enemy, from the lifelong conservative to the most ardent nationalist, here now is the window to come together in consultation and in this first, vital step that we cannot bypass to regain this republic.

Chapter 6: Forging Nationalism – Slow Road to Culture

An argument I've been making with increasing tenacity is cultural nationalism is the necessary step between the two arguing sides of civic nationalism and ethnic nationalism, the reconciliation and bridge between two visions which are far less incompatible than their loudest voices argue. To prove why, we need to reach an understanding about what culture is and how it is created.

Thinking about culture, we think about the ideas, values, and themes that define nations and civilizations alike, and which are internalized in the citizenry as part of their identity as well as promoted by both public and private institutions as a source of pride. We think of areas like art, music, and literature as essential to culture, but when we distinguish a culture, we have a certain flavor in mind that unites disparate forms and expression under common tropes.

Western Civilization had a clear sense of culture. It began with the ancient cultures of Greece and Rome, of exploration of the mind, the role of man in state and society, and in the foundation of law and knowledge to build a better future. Christianity was introduced to the ancient world to create the ethics of our medieval age which embraced faith, love, and charity, building upon and extending existing Pagan traditions. The Enlightenment offered the opportunity to add science and reason in greater measure, as we balanced our love for our fellow men with the desire to understand the world in greater depth and detail. By the early

Twentieth Century, we had explored nature, beauty, truth, reason, and faith in grand detail and claimed each of these as elements of our cultural mix, leading to wonderful works of art, engineering, and societies where states reflected different national tastes under a broadly dominant global civilization, the envy of the world and in a preeminent position.

But culture has its discontents, and the Marxists, as is often their case, use their perpetual promises of equality to destroy quality and that which is beautiful. Their communist revolution in Russia and the socialism they encouraged throughout not just Europe but Asia, Africa, and Latin America has taken hundreds of millions of lives, a full order of magnitude beyond even the worst figures attributed to nationalism, and yet because these same Marxists ensured their control over the media and education, we hear nary a scant word about the deaths from Lenin, Stalin, Mao, Pol Pot, or innumerable others. According to the Left, they were merely misguided, but their ideas weren't bad. If you want to believe that, go visit Venezuela and try to find a meal.

The Marxists redefine truth. They pervert your truth into relativism, and then attack you whenever you try to speak out for your morality. They purchase the media which then attacks you further, and they use the law to persecute you, creating protected classes of all groups who help them and hate crimes where the guilty can be considered especially guilty if and only if they belong to a proscribed identity, almost always the majority and the classes who defend traditional sources of authority.

My first book, *Someone Has to Say It*, details their rampage over the last hundred years in exhaustive detail, but for our purposes here it is sufficient to say they targeted the following groups: They intentionally radicalized women against men, using sex as a weapon to destroy the traditional family, setting men and women at odds with one another, and casting their children adrift for the state to now educate. They radicalized minorities, whom they brought here in numbers beyond any potential ability to assimilate, knowing their divergent cultures would clash with the existing Western values. Foremost among those impacted are Christians, who despite overwhelmingly practicing a policy of love, tolerance, and nonviolence, have somehow been transformed into hateful bigots by a complicit and deceitful media.

Up has literally become down, and that's what the Marxists have done to our culture. They have turned men into women, gays into normalcy, Muslims into peaceful residents, and argue sincerely that we are the crazy ones for following our natural instincts to defend what anyone with any sense of reason or morality would realize quickly must be the foundation of any lasting civilization: The family and the community. We are called hateful for defending mothers and fathers, and told nationalism is the root of hate, because it is the one force which best unites families in common cause in defense of virtue and shared survival.

We know the values that brought us to success, because despite their many efforts to erase and rewrite our past, the Internet has opened whole areas for discussion, observation, and debate which were hidden to all but the most persistent researcher for many years. We can see how our ancestors built these great nations and world spanning empires, how they created the innovations which power our world, and we discern in their art and architecture a confident and assured people who had faith in their own capacities.

Western Civilization has striven, and it has achieved, overcoming all obstacles, not without conflict, but guided by a vision that a better future could be realized through using our minds, following our traditional morality, and with faith in each other and in our Creator. And now, for too many of our people, we've lost that awareness, and allowed our civilization to languish in the hands of lesser intellects who see only what they can take, or the guilt we should feel, instead of remembering there was a vision here once. For America specifically, we were once the indispensable nation, our destiny manifest, and no frontier was beyond our ability to tame. We are the children of two great legacies, from the European motherland and from the American wilderness, with the bravest people of many nations who came here in hope of opportunity and achievement.

Let me pause here because I know how I am defining this culture sounds like it could be very inclusive. To be fair, I know there are individuals from every civilization who could benefit by being Americans, and from whom America could benefit. But culture is sticky, and the point we sometimes miss is when we bring in people from other cultures, is that they come with their own ideas that will also shift how we think. If we bring in a few people to a well-defined and confident America, within a generation or two, they may become good Americans. My own Polish and

Russian ancestors, along with Irish and Italians did this to join the White Anglo-Saxon Protestant majority, and I'm aware it was contentious. But the commonalities, to be blunt, were many: White Europeans largely of Christian extraction came here without welfare to work and worship. Now, things are different.

We bring in people at random, giving preference to the least successful people on Earth, inviting them, as Trump rightly notes, to dump those people others do not want here in America. We see how our government, at different levels, has proven only too happy with their nonprofit allies to sprinkle them throughout our nations, creating seedbeds of crime and chaos in what were otherwise safe areas. The statistics are out there to be found, and they don't lie. Bring in people who have a different religion, a different culture, and most importantly, in the absence of a culture which could even try to integrate them, and you cause the entire country to regress. America, sadly, has undergone these changes.

We are a less cultured people than we were just three generations ago. When you look at videos from the Forties, Fifties, or early Sixties, you see a country united, where racial differences were being bridged, minorities uplifted under a secure and helpful majority, and where we could enjoy the same music and art, even as different groups participated to add unique styles to shared forms. It was a safe America, a healthier America, and one where the family was the center of life and optimism was abundant.

Had that America continued without the disruption of the later Sixties and Seventies, imagine where we would be today! We would be much more united, not having taken in so many people from foreign lands, and instead of hearing the Left agitate about the plight of minorities, our far smaller African and Native American populations would be integrated, and the enormous Latino migration would still largely be south of the border. There would be political arguments, but they would be about the size and scope of the welfare state instead of the existential struggle we now slide deeper into each day between peoples – defined by their divergent and incompatible cultures – which was pushed onto us by a wicked few and an ignorant mass.

I won't lie. I'm livid when I look at the America we lost. For a long time, I hated Baby Boomers who, by all appearances to people my age and younger, seem to have just given this away. But after talking to many people, I've come to realize they were lied to also, and many were just trying to do the right thing. They bought the story of equality, and that is how they killed our culture.

So, how do we rebuild the culture? We start by admitting that equality is not only an unachievable goal, it is an undesirable one. We aim for supremacy – American supremacy – taking the best people we have here, strengthening the existing majority with those from without who have the most to contribute, and actively standing against those who threaten those of us who want to build. We cannot co-exist with Marxism, and we need to retake our schools, our media, and restore the institutions of civic life. Government can and must help, but this project is going to take generations to achieve, and we need to recognize this before we begin if we hope to succeed.

Better laws and better leadership will demonstrate to the American people that the way of life our forefathers once envisioned is not dead. I cannot say how our government will need to evolve to accomplish these ends, but I would note as a nationalist, our guiding principle in governance should be how to work for the betterment of our people – those who are citizens, who share our beliefs and our ancestry, and to be creative in accomplishing these ends. We should work to restore the best of the old but be open to creative interpretations of the new that enhance our traditions and bolster our nature.

It's a strangely ironic reality that this is already happening. If you do not understand the world of memes, or maybe missed the dynamic creativity of the Alt-Right, perhaps because the media told you to be afraid, you're missing out on a rebirth of Western idealism into the Information Age. Unlike the stale censors of the Left who fear knowledge and history with the revelation of their perpetual misdeeds and failures, those of us brave enough to speak out are having some of the best, deepest, and most important conversations had in a century. We turn sacred cows into hamburger, and we ask the questions that matter, like what is this life and how do we make it mean something once more.

For our courage, we are placed on lists, attacked by thugs, and listed as hate groups. But as with anything else in this Orwellian inversion, the reality is those speaking out now are acting out of a deep and profound love for our heritage and our potential, with respect for others, and in love of our own people. I love America. I love New England. I love being White. I love the West. I'll fight for any of these, but to tell you the truth, I hope to fight for each, because each for their own reasons, is worth saving.

People say with good cause that politics is downwind from culture. We see this in how the Left operates and how their adherents are indoctrinated in the public-school system and then in the universities and the big corporations where they use the Human Resource Departments as their own internal surveillance to monitor compliance. They can do this because they control the legacy media, both on television and in print, and they're trying to co-opt the Internet the same way. To their eternal shame, major social media platforms like Facebook, Google, Apple, and Twitter are gladly working alongside them, and even as we migrate at the speed of light to places where we may speak freely such as Gab, OneWay, Voat, and DuckDuckGo, we should not allow these cartels to simply exist. We can use government to break their monopolies just as they would to us.

But the corollary to culture being upwind of politics is that laws and habits create culture. If you doubt this, think about your own employment. Are there certain jokes that you can appreciate specific to your field of expertise that would be shared between everyone who does your profession? Did the habits and experiences of a lifetime, mandated from above, shape what you find to be funny, what you find to be proper, and how you carry yourself as a social being both in your professional capacity and without? Can you see how law plays the same role in inspiring culture, and over the course of years and decades, how the consistent application of a certain set of beliefs creates the desire to express those ideas and ideals in other ways?

America was once a country with weak laws and a strong culture, and it worked because the culture itself mandated the habits which allowed us to enjoy such liberties without the heavy hand of the state. Now, we are a country with a divided culture, but strong laws. We have regressed, perhaps to use the best analogy, to a set of tribes who are in search of a leader with enough authority to unite us again into something better. We remember what we once had, we know where we want to go, but we need a strong government now to reclaim what we once had without government, because our enemies are now without and within.

It's beyond the scope of this volume, but I have so many conversations about hierarchy and authority, asking if our government has taken on the right responsibilities, and how deeply we need to have the state reach into our lives to ignite the cultural flame once more. I don't know the answer to these important questions, although my personal tendency is to argue for more authority, clearly defined in scope, but I also know the more people who awaken to these discussions and participate, the stronger our culture will be and the more liberty we can enjoy. We need responsible people who exercise their citizenship actively, and not who cower in fear of speaking out because of social consequence from bullies who in most cases couldn't even throw a punch. Consider who we allow to frighten us for just a moment and see them as the paper tigers they are: Well-funded, but paper thin, and whose instincts are merely to complain and steal.

We can do better, and cultural nationalism is the first evolution we need to seek as we expand upon the civic nationalism we on the Right all support as the original step toward putting America first once more. What we must remember as civic nationalism evolves is that we must be willing to hold one another to account, because if we allow half our people to live under the opposite set of values, then we are nothing but a people divided, and we will fail to ever advance toward the stability and better life we so earnestly desire. We must also disabuse ourselves of the foolish and cowardly notion that if we just ignore them and live our lives, they will live and let live.

For better or worse, that approach was tried by the conservative movement to give the cultural Left the tolerance they claimed would suffice, and I ask you to consider how they have behaved upon being given everything they wanted and then some. They became spoiled, entitled, hostile, and now use the law and violence, as much as they can, to force the rest of us into compliance with their worldview.

It is an ugly thing, perhaps, but nations cannot exist overly long when divergent visions of truth compete with one another. They have theirs, will fight for it, and will kill for it. We need a culture that is cognizant of those facts, strong enough to fight and win battles against such, but still moral enough to bring together people in common cause as we must. It has always been and will always be harder to organize our side because the Right likes to think, and we have strong opinions. I know better than to attempt to dissuade you on the many issues where you disagree with me, as you must, but instead argue facing this imminent crisis, that we might unite together to take back what is in peril, and to hold those who push these ideas we can all agree are wrong to common account.

We have been trained to look the other way and consider it good manners. But honestly, it is a culture of weakness, and as Trump demonstrates each day, a strong America is a successful America. We honor his leadership, the latest and greatest in a long line stretching back to our Founders and before, when we show our willingness to stand for our beliefs without apology and without quarter for those who think they can steal from us what we fairly earned, possess, and develop. As we become stronger, we will see their weakness, and denuded of their bought lobbies, rhetorical tricks, and unsavory guilt, American pride will arise as the foundation of a better culture, stronger for having overcome their challenge.

Achieving that culture is just a matter of will, effort, and energy. For too long, we've accepted mediocrity as the best we can manage, but I think in our hearts, each of us knows we have more to contribute. I know all too well because I allowed myself to settle into a quiet life of contemplation rather than choosing these battles, and yet, I was less than I could have been as that man. Now, for better or worse, this person who is unafraid to speak out is who I truly am, and I want our culture and our country back. Do you feel the same?

A day will come when institutions exist once more to protect our land, where people of faith and character are no longer assaulted, and we no longer have our thought leaders preaching self-hatred. If you really think about it, what we tolerate now is unnatural for our culture, and so, as we assert ourselves and hold ourselves and each other to account, we will find the restoration will at least begin far more swiftly than anyone now believes possible. There is a hunger and thirst for meaning and depth, and once those gatekeepers have been removed, the energies already spilling over the surface will break through and usher America into a new age of prosperity, hope, and ambition.

Chapter 7: Nationalism Realized – How Identity Becomes Ethnicity

If I asked you to define what makes a nation, many would answer by explaining that nations are groups of people who share certain common characteristics and shared identity, most commonly language, region, familial bonds, and from those, ethnicity under a common race and heritage. You could think of a nation, in this context, as people who have traveled a similar path for so long that their destinies and families have become so intertwined that it becomes impossible to separate them from each other, and they've stopped being mere tribes and have instead become something greater.

The origin of ethnic groups isn't something commonly discussed these days where the idea in vogue is to treat the formation of identity, save as a hostile subgroup against a regressive majority, as anathema, but we can look at nearly any European country and see how our ancestors were brought together from small squabbling tribes to the great nations of historical accounts.

Let's use the United Kingdom, our most direct ancestor in terms of legality if not always ethnicity, as an example. Historical England is very much a polyglot nation, combing Norman nobility from France, Viking raiders and their offspring, Saxon farmers, and Celtic and Gaelic warrior people with just a hint of Roman laws and odds and ends. We can pull out each individual thread that makes up the English identity, let alone the complications of being British, but what we find is common residency in an area, shared beliefs, a solid legal system, a common faith, and maybe most importantly, shared battles against external threats, took these mostly complementary yet sometimes different peoples and ideas and forged them into something new: England. Ironically, France was shaped in a similar fashion, in concert with and in opposition to England, as the Hundred Years War defined for both what their nations would be beyond the kings and their armies who waged combat.

Regrettably, that England might be fading into the annals of history, at least in London, as the government of that country, like so many others in the West, seems to be willfully acting in contradiction of its own history as they bring in people whose identity is stronger than what they can now preserve at home. As stated earlier, the egalitarians and globalists see this as a desired feature of immigration, because to make new bonds of loyalty to their despotic future state, they know they must first destroy all existing bonds of kinship to mitigate the risk of future revolt.

Perhaps the Left learned this lesson from the fall of their beloved Soviet Union. Considering how the Cold War dominated the international narrative for half a century, it's curious how the whole affair seemed to end with a whimper, a short-lived triumph on one side, and then faded into history. We saw the Soviet state collapse, first shedding peripheral nations like Poland and Hungary who had comparatively strong national identity, but then we saw constituent states like Ukraine and Belarus emerge shortly thereafter from what had been parts of the Russian Empire which predated communism by many years. For the many years, the Leftists had followed the Stalinist model of socialism in one country, using force to subdue individual nations rather than the global uprising which Marx predicted, and which best fulfills their rhetorical dreams. But what they discovered in the failure of the USSR is that nationalism lurked just beneath the surface and along with a resurgent faith which put to shame the sham equality which was the best they could muster, that nations could and would emerge from their failed leadership. Nationalism proved remarkably immune to their false promises.

Living in the moment, it's always difficult as a historian to assess what trends are happening, but it seems increasingly likely that the struggle between Left and Right, between equality and quality, or those who distribute versus those who contribute, is being realized in this era not between two superpowers, but instead between the globalist faction that seeks to force humanity to unite under one banner against we nationalists who seek to preserve our distinctions. What we certainly know is that the Left has worked decisively and unremittingly to destroy national sovereignty everywhere it is allowed, and we know that as part of that process they've sought to unmake the integrity of peoples through the illogical introduction of foreign elements.

Worth noting here, since I know this book will be accused of being a hateful screed and then derided as such by people who lack the courage to even confront the ideas contained within, is that referring to outsiders as undesirable is not inherently any comment against their character or value as people. I assume most people are decent, with a few bad ones everywhere, and a few good ones as well, but recognize also that cultures shape people in different patterns with widely variant expectations. As such, even good people of sound mind and true belief introduced to a foreign civilization might be a bad fit. We're not supposed to state the obvious fact that apples and oranges don't always mix, and while nationalists have an obvious solution to this in keeping the fruits separated by clearly delineated borders, the globalists deliberately conflate the two and use their rhetoric and coercion to deter people from speaking against this. So, in asserting that not all immigrants are a good fit, or more basically that every nation's primary and singular obligation is to its own people, I make this statement based on love for my people and not hatred of the other.

All that made clear, we begin to see the path by which an American ethnicity might become a reality. To build an ethnicity, just as one would construct any meal, there needs to be a basic ingredient upon which it is composed. For America, should we wish to preserve our history, heritage, and traditions, and to see these renewed, the only real choice is to recognize White identity at the heart of future endeavors, as it is the European traditions in both thought and practice which are necessary to sustain the rule of law upon which we rely, far more than other nations, and which link us both with our history and with the culture proven to be most compatible with the institutions the civic nationalists seek to defend and secure. As Whites remain the majority in this country with over 60% of the population, and equally relevant, as well over 90% of the voting Right, we are functionally already united upon this basis and are only hindered by our unwillingness, for fear of labeling or persecution, to voice the obvious: The Right essentially is White America.

If you doubt this contention, close your eyes and picture a generic group of Democrats and a generic group of Republicans. What did you see? If your mental imagery is anything close to the actual demographics, the Left would be a polyglot mixture of people with little in common in core beliefs save for a unifying hatred against their opposition. The Right, by contrast, would be overwhelmingly though not exclusively White, but very much similar in appearance, style, and how they present themselves publicly.

It's considered highly impolitic to be so blunt and honest, but given the demographic realities, and our expressed desire both to regain civic integrity and spawn cultural renewal, we can no longer pretend to ignore whole groups and their patterns of behavior. We can, and we should recognize individuals who deviate from those patterns for better or worse. But to allow entire groups to escape sanction when they work so overwhelmingly against our purposes is one of the worst opportunities we've permitted the Left and it must end if we are to survive. When we virtue signal to their idea of group identity, where certain people are held both above and beyond sanction, that is profoundly unhealthy and dangerous because it encourages the very cultural divisions they use to regress the state to a point where their naked power grab is supported by their ever-growing segments of our population.

Ethnic nationalists reading these arguments will already understand the need for common genetic ancestry to ensure familial loyalties unite people in common cause. Where they may take umbrage is in the next part, which I believe will be an essential part of the American equation as opposed to Europe, which is that among those minorities who adopt our culture, our values, and our way of life, there is some room for integration and assimilation.

To use the cooking metaphor once more, once the main dish has been constructed, different people might choose to flavor the main dish to suit. Some will prefer to keep things bland and just enjoy the basic construction of a dinner. Conversely, some might choose to add a dash of salt, pepper, a condiment or the like. With full recognition such a strong flavor has a disproportionate impact, unless the basic dish is undesirable to one's taste on its own merit, most people choose to use these accessory flavors sparingly as they can overwhelm and ruin what otherwise would be a most excellent dish.

As well as any, this metaphor explains the balance between minorities and a majority in national construction. As the number of minorities grow, their desire for power will invariably and predictably grow, destroying the integrity of the previously extant nation, leading most often toward the zero-sum game whereby sides are forced to fight one another for dominance. There is little formal research of which I am aware on where the tipping point rests, but it seems to me based upon watching how individual states and cities shift hard Left, about the time the majority population falls under 80%, between the combination of Whites who defect to the Left to assuage their guilt and the growing and radicalized minority base proves populous enough to sustain single party rule by the Left. That's why they control most of our cities, and because minorities mostly vote uniformly for their idea to redistribute our holdings, they never lose control of the Democrat cities despite going on over a hundred years of failure in some circumstances.

Perversely, the more Republicans succeed, the more Democrats become envious, which is why economic growth only accelerates cultural warfare, and this is why the Marxists shifted their focus from economics to culture, as it allowed them to subvert our actions to their intent just as readily as they would use their own periods of control to prepare for ultimate victory by constantly expanding those spheres into which government impacts our lives. They're clever in the most devious of ways, which is why to defeat them, we need to not only attack their ideas and institutions but be certain to remove people who are overwhelmingly prone to support their ideology from our midst as quickly and humanely as we can. We will discuss this in far greater detail when we consider immigration and citizenship, but should we adopt the public goal of protecting our heritage, history, and rule of law, we need to recognize the inherent liability of the foreign element to that struggle.

A stronger culture and stronger government are more able to integrate and assimilate foreign elements into the primary cultural, national, and eventually, ethnic construct. Those of us on the Right flank who have spent time thinking about these problems honestly rather than conceding victory to the Left by refusing to call a spade a spade, will all tell you we can't simply have open doors to anyone and everyone anymore. Where we disagree is how far we can go in integration and assimilation, with some people making strong arguments that to have any but the slightest foreign element among a people is leaving a door open to future strife along the same lines we experience today, while others still suggest moral tests whereby we can determine the commitment of any given citizen to the national culture, recognizing both in majority and minority alike, having a fifth column within to spread dissent and division is highly detrimental.

That's another reason why, as we consider this mature stage of how we form a nation, recognizing that our institutions have been broken and how multiculturalism has shattered our consensus, there's an increasing appreciation for having more authoritarian forms of government to provide the sort of clarity and unity which democracy simply does not permit. Absent strong laws and strong leadership, if politics is allowed to shift back and forth between such dissimilar ideologies as what we want on the Right and the nihilism of the Left, it will be impossible to rebuild or preserve what remains of our culture, and agreeing to fight on those terms is just a slow-motion surrender to their demographic assault.

Knowing that nationalism does not mesh well with democracy, that's why the globalists push so hard to preserve democracy everywhere they can, because it works to allow them to divide nations who lack the cultural maturity or unity to even consider such a system. They like that it puts constant strife and division at the heart of our political discourse and given how much money they possess and are willing to spend, they can constantly shift coalitions to ensure no effective opposition arises to forestall their planned usurpation.

In the coming years, I think we will see much more discourse on the Right about what the best form of government might be, with the minimal reset point being the recognition our Founders intended a Republic which was far less swayed by the immediate passions of all these perpetual lobbies, and which had many built-in safeguards against the very situation we face today, where we've now reached that point where the collapse is imminent because the majority have learned how to use government to take from the productive minority. Once people have gone that far in corruption, it's worth asking, as a sincere question, whether we do more harm than good to have people govern themselves in terms of their momentary wants versus a system with more layers of protection to ensure those leaders selected are not the most skillful politicians, but instead men of experience and learning who will consider the long-term needs of the entire nation.

Such men, who took this responsibility seriously, played a vital role in the formation of European national identity, and we should deeply consider what service an elite could provide that did not embrace globalism and the erasure of our sovereignty and cultural beliefs, but instead took its very mission, it's purpose of state, to be the defense and rebuilding of the nation. Given the widespread apathy of our citizenry at large and given also the clear failure of democracy to do anything but create the demand for something resembling effective leadership, I think the question we're going to end up asking is in whom we invest the power to fix this.

I know that might also be a hard pill to swallow for people who love the Constitution and limited government, and I do also. But as the Founders themselves knew, the people themselves, if given a system better than their ability to manage, will only drive themselves into corruption even more quickly. These things are cyclical, and even as we recognize and celebrate the foresight with which our national investiture was launched, we also must be honest that for some time now, we've seen the erosion of our legal protections, and the Left's voter replacement and radicalization strategy has killed our ability to sustain America as it was originally designed.

We can and should argue about the way forward, built upon the goal of preventing the Left from removing our people or our ideals from dominance, and rejecting their specious arguments, because they brought in a bunch of outsiders without ever seeking anything resembling national consent to their scheme. Their voices should not carry equal weight versus those who have been here longer, who arrived legally, and whose families are most invested. We must recognize in ourselves that we must serve as the agents of the restoration. While we welcome those here, especially citizens, who want to serve as allies to this great cause, it is we who must remain the motor by which the restoration is accomplished.

As we do that, our struggle will forge our unity in support of common values and the cultural foundations that will, over a few generations, define what it means to be American in a way where we too become our own ethnicity. Those who look differently than us will be integrated, and those who think differently than us on our core values will become marginalized and removed from being able to harm or oppress us any further.

When we abandon diversity, tolerance, and multiculturalism as the cultural ideas, we will embrace their opposites: unity, values, and a common culture. Read those options closely and ask which you think most likely to endure, and which you would not only want for your children and loved ones, but which will allow them to succeed for many generations henceforward into the future. I concede the Left's values make for an easier short-term effort, as they exist in a place beyond effort, judgment, or care. But isn't that precisely how we lost so much in the first place?

To build a nation, strong laws and leadership is needed, from which culture arises, and through which identity becomes a force for union instead of division. The question of how we get there is an exercise of will, identifying honestly and openly which people and which ideas should gain social currency. While there must always be room for disagreement and dissent, and a degree of tolerance for those who diverge occasionally, there must also be an awareness that such flexibility can no longer give way to the licentiousness and relativism prevalent today. For if we are not forceful in asserting our beliefs and our identity, who else will stand for us?

These last three chapters reconcile the different strands of nationalism in the common concern of people looking out for their own welfare on a principled basis. The last question remaining, which will be how we distinguish ourselves, and through which America and any other nation must be defined, is what values do we hold most dear? We haven't allowed ourselves to ask that question in a very long time because we feared the fight it would cause among ourselves. But, now that the fight is already upon us, there's no better time to ask ourselves: just what are we willing to fight to achieve, and what might inspire us to victory?

Chapter 8: The Values that Build a Nation

Ideology took primacy in political discourse because it is convenient to define and divide the world into categories where behaviors can be predicted according to existing systems. As systems tend to remain in place from day-to-day, such system-based logic works well for describing many behaviors within a state, but if you break these philosophies down even deeper, there exists at the core only two types of values: Transactional and non-transactional.

Starting with transactional values, we recognize the most likely state of society is for people to trade a given idea, object, or service without constraints other than those voluntarily adopted. Less awkwardly, our tendency is when we have something, we're inclined to trade and talk about whatever this interest is, in the absence of strong social inducements not to do so. From these values come our economics, finance, and the world of business.

What distinguishes civics, culture, and ultimately nations are those values which are exempted from the market in that they voluntarily assign added importance, ranging from elevated consideration to having certain values be considered sacrosanct. For the purposes of developing a national identity, these are the values which will matter most, because it is these exceptions which represent the distinctive characteristics of a certain people.

How these develop is an incredible process that deserves far greater consideration as nationalism becomes better articulated. The most commonly shared values seem to be those which emerge from our natural instincts, such as to seek out partnership between a man and a woman, that children deserve protection, that our departed loved ones be remembered, and that those who sacrifice for the good of all should be venerated. Although these values are under assault today in what is an historical oddity and likely to prove an unusual dispute, the idea that care and concern for one's loved ones and closest kin should be at the center of our political world harmonizes basic human instincts with political expression. Such resonance plays a key role in why the nation has endured so long, because unlike other abstract entities that might work better on paper, the nation exists as the eventual extension of the family itself.

If you accept that the well-designed state seeks to allow for the fulfillment of the most people in seeking out their own individual happiness, one would think putting these sorts of innate values at the center of designing or restoring a nation would be the most obvious first step, but what's both astounding and disappointing is that when we argue about politics, we so often retreat to speaking of ideology and infrastructure, or discussing the merits of some limited policy plan. Beyond using certain buzz words that have been spoken so frequently by those who primarily have a terrible track record of embodying the words they deliberately abuse, it seems like neither the market nor the state driven value systems have the means to express care for what the people themselves desire.

Where this becomes even more interesting, as well as contentious, is how we define those values which are not strictly driven by biological imperative, but instead are developed from years of cultural or educational effort. These values are usually rooted in our history, as with our Western traditions of inquiry, innovation, industry, and integrity. It often works out that we lose sight of the reason why we do such things or believe such things to the passing ages of history, but the lessons learned from our experiences shape a collective lens through which each nation observes the world slightly differently.

The ranking of these values is a question we rarely ask, but without which we seem sometimes unable to clearly explain our world. We've succumbed to the disease of moral relativism which renders our judgments slurred, as we cannot make clear distinctions about health and sickness, in nations just as in the social habits of people. As we disagree about who we are as a people, due to the cultural divisions which are just a broader categorization for these core non-transactional values, we find that the values themselves lose social currency and we descend toward the lowest common denominator where everything is treated as fungible.

Most ideologues working within the current paradigm that tends to pit the state versus the market, concern themselves primarily with power and how to amass authority over as many series of transactions as possible, taking a functionalist view of politics and society. Conversely, the nationalist, starting from the foundation of satisfying the popular well-being, needs to put much more energy into clarifying those beliefs which will bind the nation together and upon which the political effort made shall receive its primary thrust.

As they are always evolving, the non-transactional values which bring together a nation will inherently be a source of dispute, but what we find increasingly in America is that our institutions seem only to offer a highly slanted version which comports not with the clearly expressed traditions and the intent of those who created this nation, both at its inception and through the many generations since, but instead with a radical fringe element obsessed with a profoundly unnatural form of egalitarianism that destroys all other values beyond this: Equality must be realized by whatever means necessary.

If that is a crass oversimplification of Leftist belief, it's also the simplest explanation which can be shared that accurately reflects their practice across different nations and scenarios. There's much to be said for simplicity when considering values, because while we obviously must defend a great many things we hold dear and which we would not want to trade away, determining what is most precious to people is how we learn who we really are. Part choice, part chance, and part inheritance, that question is the vital one which nationalists must develop.

Trump's articulation of Make America Great Again fits the prescription incredibly well because of how succinctly it conveys a few powerful ideas. The essential optimism about our past and our future is bound up in a challenge and call to arms which appeals to the largest number possible, at least at the rhetorical level before getting caught in the inevitable weeds of policy. But within marketing clever terminology, one could also pull out words like renaissance, restoration, and revival – a remembrance of what America was and the resolve to make it into something again rather than simply trying to be.

American identity, uniquely in comparison to our European counterparts as well as most other national experiences, is caught up in the process of doing things rather than being something. Owing at least partly to our novelty as a nation and the relative youth of our history, part of our story is going to be about ethics and aspirations, and when well-employed this sort of mission-based nationalism can contribute much to ambition and stability.

It's like when a person works on a team to accomplish a goal larger than themselves, sometimes what emerges beyond the momentary struggle of whatever objective is presented ends up being more important. Well-chosen values draw many people to their support and defense, and as those people organically connect with one another for individual benefit, that's how the mutual benefit of a common culture can be finally restored. Which values do we choose and how do we prioritize them?

To enjoy popular support, we start with the nationalist ideal we could call folkism, a series of levels of hierarchy that put families first and see communities and all other evolved social levels as extensions from the nuclear family outwards, making loyalty and commonality the aspiration in how we relate to one another – creating a society based on relationships rather than the transaction monitoring preferred by both the market and state centric models.

Given the challenges we face, any nation that hopes to overcome the assault by cultural Marxism will also need to have the most forceful argument against their values of equality, profligacy, and dependency, so our aspirations to counter them most directly and effectively must be quality, standards, and independence. To overlook this challenge, as our nation did for so many years, will ensure cultural Marxist voices remain dominant, but even if an alternative paradigm emerges, leaving them unchecked will only hasten the return of their lunacy. Considering how destructive they've proven time and again throughout the history of our entire civilization, it seems like the time has arrived when we must confront them in order to save ourselves, and most importantly, we must destroy their ideas with superior alternatives.

So, who are we? America must become the nation where family comes first, where we examine every value and make intelligent choices for the benefit of our people, looking for the best life can offer, holding ourselves and our fellow citizens to account, and allowing for optimal liberty beyond these values we hold most dear. Our future sounds a lot like our past, but such a clear description of the charge we must undertake also reveals that what matters most are not the systems of governance, or what power is designated to what level, but rather determining through which means we can best preserve our values rather than the old functionalist approach.

If we start with a values-based approach, the logical way to proceed to ensure national unity, a positive force for state stability and a morally sound path based upon securing popular sovereignty as a long-term option, is to place the promotion of those values most important to the society at the center of government. This is an inversion of how the Founders thought about the fledgling American republic, which makes this divergence worth deeper discussion.

When America was founded, people lived very much apart from one another and had limited ability to have much intentional impact upon others. Government was incredibly weak, so the individual functionally enjoyed a greater impact over their own life than modern society could easily allow without breaking down over its own contradictions. As government now enjoys so much more authority, which is an expectation of the people who are going to prove amenable again and again to using government to fulfill their expectations of value fulfillment and for the protection of society, we too must accept that values are going to emerge as much outward from the center as upward from the individual.

Importantly, a well-designed system by Right thinking individuals will, as our Founders themselves wisely chose, secure certain liberties to individuals in defense of their values where we would not want government to have undue intrusion. But, the balance lies in the realization that we need government to help secure our culture, and to both preserve and rebuild unity. These responsibilities should be gauged one-by-one to see if they make the most sense to be handled at either Federal, State, or more local levels.

As the traditional Republican position has been to devolve power to the lowest level based upon the idea that individual sovereignty is most essential to our well-being, shifting power upward to more central levels of authority will be challenging. But without a common culture, which is shaped so heavily by media, by education, and by the sorts of ideas that should unite a nation but are sadly now used to divide our country, the only state that can survive is one whose sole sanction is force and compliance, precisely where the Left wants us to go.

None of us want that, so instead we should deeply examine if we have the right values at the right levels. We want our most dearly held beliefs to have great protection at the individual level, but to also have forceful advocacy at the national level. For those other values which should be traded as people are encouraged to explore the range of options in those areas where there is no cultural or national threat and where free expression advances knowledge and understanding, those are the places where we should revert power to the lowest level possible, including the individual.

Unfortunately, we now have a state that increasingly regulates the wrong areas more intrusively, attacking the liberties we would like to preserve, while slipping into areas of life where there is no reason for our rights to be so infringed. This fits the Left's value structure of centralizing all decision making, which we should oppose in favor of centralizing only those ideas most important. What we would offer is a strong central government, but with a clearly defined role and scope, constrained within the boundaries of law, and designed specifically to benefit the family and individuals therein.

Naturally, there will be much discussion about what problems should be solved at what level, but it's not a discussion we've had too often on the Right. We've always talked about the question of responsibility, not from the moral perspective of satisfying popular needs, but instead from the legal perspective of what the Constitution requires. It's a good place to start and I do not glibly suggest we simply adopt the ideal of absolute power, as that would not work for our people and would abandon our best traditions and our own expectations. But I do recognize there are times when we need to be willing to use government to accomplish the ends our people desire. Conservatism might have identified these as a sell-out, based on the idea that markets should govern many areas, but nationalists would recognize that by meeting the legitimate needs of our people, our moral position becomes more secure and our people more united.

If America First is people first, tempered by wisdom and the limits of what can be functionally accomplished, I think values-based nationalism, the cultural component which strengthens and builds upon civic pride, is a place we can go together, and as we come to celebrate 250 years in the coming decade, we can re-chart the course for this American project such that hopefully centuries later, our descendants will learn from how we overcame this vital challenge.

We could go into much more detail on other abstract values, but instead of taking that approach, let's build off the obvious traits of nationalism, the defense of a well-defined group of people based upon shared morality and identity, and look how we could apply this sort of thinking, with respect for the individual and their liberty and autonomy, but also the willingness to approach authority with a more flexible stance, to develop a policy agenda. Instead of limiting our vision here to what would be easiest to sell, such a framework gives us sanction to look at what must be done to fulfill these goals, both considering our own beliefs and the need for self-preservation, but also in light of how this intention will most likely be subverted.

Now, with the understanding of what nationalism is, how it evolves, and how it is necessary for Right thinkers and the Republican Party to compete, we can start making honest assessments about where our interests and values lie, and develop a policy platform that can be both populist and effective in thwarting the Left's long-standing agenda to overtake this country.

Chapter 9: Immigration – A Country Is Its People

There can be no question of greater significance to the nationalist than who is and who is not a member of the nation. Starting with the bare minimum requirements, it seems obvious that no person who lacks citizenship should be considered as having equal standing regarding matters of the state. Such a statement would have been incredibly basic and non-controversial just a few years ago, but we've literally reached a point where phrases like "undocumented citizens" are used to masquerade the slow-motion invasion which our policy makers have welcomed over the previous decades.

The presumption that America automatically owes anything to the world beyond taking care and concern for our own citizens and acting responsibly and peacefully with other nations is ridiculous. For too long, we've accepted the propaganda that every cause, at least every cause favored by the Left, is our national dilemma, and this insane overreach has been both costly abroad in how we have been brought into conflict and calamity, and in how we have allowed our social fabric to become tattered by outside influence. When suffering happens elsewhere in this world, it is not our responsibility to take care of those who are victims as ongoing national policy.

Our job as a country is to take care of the millions of American citizens who have pressing needs here, before a dime is spent on an outsider. Because our government cares more about reaching people outside their control than honoring those to whom their service was promised, it's easy for the state to simply forget that any legitimacy our government has extends from its ability and willingness to serve our wants and needs. There are plenty of people suffering from expensive problems, from health issues to the needs of veterans, and from unhealthy drinking water to drug addictions. Every penny we spend for a service to assist an illegal migrant, or even to bring in a legal applicant, is a missed opportunity to help someone to whom we lawfully and morally owe greater consideration.

The Democrats don't truly care about our people in need, but the Republicans have said for many years that they were not our responsibility. Trump might be changing this attitude, and it's worth paying close attention to how his efforts reach across lines. A perfect example is in the way the Black community is now hearing the long overdue argument that, while the Left uses them as part of a coalition of minorities, the reality is that by bringing in huge numbers of outsiders, these new people will compete against our existing poor, draining resources from the communities impacted, and this will put our most vulnerable in close proximity with those who are the most disruptive to our society. This is what the Left calls progress, but there was a time when liberals would have had the intellectual decency to admit they were trading away their duties for votes.

Most Republicans agree that we need to stop illegal immigration, and intuitively understand that each amnesty only emboldens more people to come here to break the law. Sadly, too many of our politicians listen to the corrupting influence of the corporate lobbies who like the cheap labor and fund many campaigns, but that must end now. Not only should the Right be against illegal immigration, but we should support repatriation to the countries of origin for all people here illegally, and we should have a far more proactive system in terms of removing those who have violated their legal status to stay, as well as those who never had any papers.

With stronger enforcement measures, the southern border wall which we desperately need is but a preliminary step in a much more comprehensive series of acts we must take – not just concerning illegal immigration, but legal immigration – including people who have already come here but probably should not have been admitted.

President Trump speaks often about the basis upon which we admit immigrants – pure chance between all those whom the contributing nation allows to apply, where we basically have a lottery to receive the people least wanted in their home countries here as our new future compatriots. Our current approach to immigration would best be comparable to a sports team drafting players from a random pool that deliberately excludes the good players that the other teams want. While I'm sure some people are good who come here, the basis upon which we're making such judgment is to trust in dumb luck and to refuse to pass judgment about who would be well-suited to our country.

This is stupid. It should be opposed vigorously, and we must end the visa lottery. Furthermore, we must end the even more harmful program of chain migration. Anytime a person is granted citizenship, a door is created whereby many others can follow them to the United States as family members. This is a major contributor to how we've seen a once homogeneous country morph increasingly into collections of people who exist in their own cultures, floating across one another, but lacking the core unity which once made America both great and strong.

Trump has spoken out vigorously for these reforms as a starting point for changing our immigration system, and we must hold all Republicans to account to pass these changes. They are the bare minimum needed to stop the Left from realizing their approaching goal of taking over the country through changing demographics, and if you don't believe the imminence of this problem, do some research into which states are shifting and how the changing population of America is the core driver of this tendency. **The Coming Civil War** does this for you, showing how growth of immigrant populations far outpaces native population growth at the same time as these minority groups remain overwhelmingly radicalized by the Left against the traditions and ideals of America and her founding people.

Although Trump's suggestions are a good starting point, we need to go much further than even this, assuming the demographic numbers and voting trends don't radically change. We need fewer migrants and refugees and we need many more people who are native born and hold to our values. There are obviously two parts to that equation, and we will talk in depth about birth rates and family planning as a positive approach to this question in the next chapter, but we need to change who is coming into this country and accelerate who is leaving.

Let's start with refugees. Up until very recently, the United States was a party to an international agreement with the

United Nations whereby tens of thousands of people were placed by them into our country. Over the course of decades, hundreds of thousands of people have used this pathway combined with chain migration to put millions of people who were lightly vetted, if at all, and whose virtues and values we have no means to assess, on a path to American citizenship. To his credit, Trump has removed us from these accords, but we need to remain apart from any such treaty or compact which compels America to accept unwanted people.

The next thing we should look at is the value of legal immigration at all. We tend to ask this question in an economic context, talking about the need for migrant labor for certain low paying jobs both in service and agricultural sectors, but we ignore the cultural impact on society as a whole of having seasonal flights of labor into and out of the country, assuming it works so cleanly as that, as it often does not. History has shown it to be incredibly dangerous to rely upon outside people to do your work, and we should consider the many examples that history documents of hired hands eventually overwhelming those they once served.

Americans are a proud and industrious people who can do our own work. We should categorically reject the notion that a country with well over three hundred million people lacks for labor. If the price of having Americans build our goods, pick our fruit, and serve each other is at a premium, then let's pay it. Whatever it costs on the corporate balance sheet, we will save that cost and then some in terms of reduced social welfare, an expense which is never mentioned by the Left, but which we should never forget in our own calculations. More importantly, we will be promoting the right values of self-reliance and independence: core American values that should unite our people.

Having removed the economic basis for most migration, whether we choose to admit anyone should be a matter of the deepest consideration, and at least two traits should be required of anyone seeking entry. The first is these people should have something tangible to contribute in terms of either skills or assets. Potential alone, idealistic as it is, is not enough. Secondly, we need to have a cultural test which is honestly designed to exclude people from America whose core beliefs contradict the majority held positions of our fellow countrymen.

The Right has not been willing to take such a strong stance since probably the Eisenhower Administration launched the successful Operation Wetback to push Mexicans and other Latinos back across the border and out of our southwest. We need to do so now. And to be very clear, the choices about whom we exclude will play a major role in defining how our nation evolves to realize the goal of placing America First. We need to empower the INS to remove people who are not here legally, and to ensure they have whatever resources they require.

Nothing seems more obvious to me than excluding Muslims from further entry into the United States. The fact that our Constitution provides for freedom of speech and freedom of worship for existing citizens has been twisted into suggesting those reserved rights must be extended to foreigners, with the effect of encouraging the development of faiths which are explicitly hostile to our understanding of the world. This makes zero sense, and the instinct Trump showed in denying these people entry to our country was sound, and constituted protection we desperately need.

We do not need and do not want more people from the Third World, whose countries are only marginally functional if at all, and the cost for whom is a burden which our society cannot bear. As impolitic as it is to say, especially for non-Whites, these people overwhelmingly join the Left whose facile promises of these new entrants receiving sustenance from taking our stuff are too compelling to ignore. You see what happens in our cities, and how whole neighborhoods are transformed, and how we get pushed further to the periphery. Why would we support that?

We must be very selective in whom we bring into America in the next few years because the American values of independence, liberty, and the rule of law are at stake, because our heritage has been attacked and our culture weakened, so we cannot assimilate many people, and we cannot assimilate them easily. In truth, unless we are getting help from those we allow to migrate to this nation, we would be better served to bring in no one at all, as we already struggle to integrate those people already here. America has essentially closed its borders several times in our history, and to do so again while facing these challenges would seem most prudent.

But, if we are going to contemplate changes to immigration, what I would argue is that we need a system where we define what we want for ourselves and find only those people who will help us achieve those goals as potential new members of our society. One example which comes to mind, which is getting more publicity these days, is the sad plight of the Boers in Africa. Christian people of European extraction, they confront a government which wants to steal their land, earned and worked over generations, to fulfill a communist plot to redistribute these productive holdings to masses who have no knowledge or experience in farming the land, but who have numbers and racially motivated angst and ideology to steal that which they did not earn. People like the Boers will understand why America is special, and if anyone deserved a better chance, it would be them.

We will be called racist if we even suggest that White people belong in America. I find that whenever we can upset our enemies, just as President Trump is teaching us in how we are winning more and more, we are doing the right thing because we strengthen ourselves and weaken their claims against us. Despite what the Left claims, not only did Whites build this country, but Whites who arrive from outside America would still have much to contribute. The fact that they know this is why the one area from which people are least able to legally migrate to the United States is from other European or European settled nations. We can change this.

We need to rethink our entire approach to immigration, and to be clear, I'm not saying we will necessarily decide to shut the doors entirely to everyone somewhat unlike us. But we should be clear that we are not a dumping ground for those who are nothing like us, and it is entirely legitimate to judge potential entrants to this nation upon how well they would likely fit in with those already here. Had we the wisdom to have done this fifty years ago, how much stronger and more stable would our country be today?

Once we set the new standard for who we want and why we want them, we need to hold to these specifications and refuse to give an inch in retreat. In fact, we should discuss going further. Refugees should be repatriated to their countries of origin, especially if the chaos that caused their migration has been resolved. We should seriously discuss repealing the 1965 Hart-Cellar Act in a single swoop to remove the visa lottery and chain migration. Those who break the law on the path to citizenship, especially for violent offenses, should be gone.

If this seems harsh, please remember this: Politics as we currently play in America is nothing but a numbers game, and if we don't win, we will lose. I know our idealism is such that we want to reach people who come here because of the faith we have in our ideas, and that we have legitimate immigrant histories of our own. But consider carefully why our forefathers came here, and if by allowing these others in here now, if we are doing right by their sacrifices, or if we are putting their great project at peril. I'd argue so strongly for the latter, because I know that we must get tough on these issues or nothing else matters.

America is its people. We must choose the right ones, and recognizing the ongoing conflict, that must mean choosing only those who will support us in our effort to restore our culture, protect our liberties, and who will refuse to allow our history to be either erased or degraded. We will have to be tougher than we might want because for too many years, we were nicer than we should have been, to try to make things work. The Left, through their nonstop provocation, made integration impossible. Now, we need to be honest about that reality and all become hardliners.

Our people's security and integrity demand no less, and we should not have to hear even one more story like that of Kate Steinle, an innocent woman shot by an armed invader whom we were too timid to deport, ever again. We do this to protect our loved ones, a nation's highest and most important obligation.

Chapter 10: Family Planning – Children are the Future

As essential as controlling immigration and shifting it toward a sound and sustainable basis is, equally important to the positive flip side of this demographic equation is having a sound family planning policy. This area is one where conservatives, despite strong opinions on the subject, have largely absented themselves from public discourse and this absence must be filled if we are going to seriously rebalance who inhabits America.

There has been profound unease on the Right to speak about population and family planning since the 1940's. Any time one speaks of desirable and undesirable outcomes in terms of the people who make up society, the predictable attacks on nationalism, genocide, and family planning result. These are deliberately conflated by the media and academics in an effort to throw away some very strong ideas which are dangerous to the institutional Left with some major missteps from our own history which we must own and redress.

This volume already offered a stirring defense of nationalism as not just a valuable concept, but also the singular pathway which will restore a sense of identity and purpose to a reforged nation, able to make best use of the American state to the benefit of our people. As part of that definition, we can easily and clearly reject genocide as a legitimate policy tool, and it's worth making incredibly clear that whereas nationalism represents a model capable, under the right circumstances, of overcoming the Left/Right paradigm which we must resolve, those on the Left who accuse the Right of these acts are themselves actively perpetrating that form of population displacement and disenfranchisement against the White majority that has been the precursor to genocidal acts throughout Africa. History has shown the Left to have killed many millions more than the Right, which remains bound by our highly individual consciences. I mention all this as prologue to family planning to inoculate you from these valid but overwrought concerns.

Who has children in America and why? Let's think about the incentives and triggers that exist to encourage or discourage people from having families, first in terms of policy, but then in terms of larger social trends.

We know the state subsidizes children who have no sustenance. At this point, most people accept this situation as acceptable as few contemplate the suffering of a child as desirable. Yet, our method of dealing with this problem whereby we give money, benefits, and even elevated status to mothers who have children absent any support has consequences. When government pays for a thing, it tends to encourage it. So, we get more single mothers, more broken marriages, and more separation between men and women as the state has fundamentally inserted itself as a surrogate father to these children while demanding zero accountability and providing reliable financing. Have you ever seen how some women now seem to think of certain men this way, how their value is just in what they can financially offer and not in their ideas, their willingness to be fathers, or the unity of marriage itself as foundational?

In older days, the state frowned upon such actions, and the care for the children was taken from the mother in many cases and an orphanage or adoption was considered a better option. Without financial inducements, fewer single mothers chose to keep their children, hinting that for at least some segment, having kids is now about the money more than the family. The children were routed into the best situations possible, although there were certainly many trying situations also, but this system served to make marriage far more valuable, as our society once believed a father and mother, working in tandem, were necessary to provide mutual support and welfare for each other, as well as any children born to the couple.

Not surprisingly, when America had that model, there was neither the desire nor the need for such an expansive and intrusive welfare state, because families were able to manage these concerns mostly with genuine affection, where we now simply ask the state to intervene, so no one falls through the cracks. We're told the new system is more humane, but it's a question that bears asking. Now that we pay for unwanted kids, do we get more kids coming from people who lack resources, and is there a major social cost to this? Are kids born to single mothers more or less successful, on average, than peers who have a traditional family?

The screeching that comes from the Left on these questions hints at their importance. It turns out that children from two parent homes are far more likely to be successful than their peers, even when you account for financial differences. The state cannot make up for the lack of care and attention with any amount of money, but what they accomplish is to encourage the people with the least resources and least stable relationships to have more children than they can sustain. Do you think it any accident that the Left has used their moves in family planning to push in this direction, considering those are the exact same demographic groups which are, by far, the most likely to be their future voters?

Conversely, let's examine the situation of the nuclear two parent family which was once the social norm, but has increasingly come under attack and marginalization. As the majority of these families have greater means, they do not receive the same level of government support, if any, but instead find their tax dollars redistributed to subsidize programs which benefit not just single mothers, but integration costs of illegal immigrants, the social services they then require, and to pay for increased law enforcement presence to battle crime. The nuclear family pays into the system at such a high clip, both parents usually must work to cover their bills because they do not simply take from the state, and with such obligations, having children becomes a major cost as opposed to a benefit.

We see reinforcement of this idea in the social sphere as well. Within the mainstream media which predominantly reaches White and well-to-do populations, the language used is of sustainability and how prudent it is to not have children, to be ecologically conscious, and to give freely of one's self. Conversely, within the Black media, as one example, the culture which is put out by people who own the same platforms glorifies taking, having more for one's self, and eschews any sense of collective responsibility. We see university students being told not to have children and instead invest in their careers, or give support to the Third Worlders, at home or abroad who have far more children. What are the results?

Birth rates are taboo, but only Whites worldwide fail to reach replacement levels. Why? The combination of active propaganda which discourages our procreation, immigration policies designed to substitute more pliable foreigners for native born children, and state subsidies which benefit the least productive elements of our population at the expense of the most productive all work in combination to lead to a de-facto replacement policy. While these policies work formally on socio-economic levels, when you factor in the constant agitprop, it becomes clear that family planning in America is how the Left prevents us from renewing ourselves.

To further complicate these issues, they put additional levels of confusion above the disconnect they encourage for the nuclear family. Their encouragement of feminism, and the way in which Courts basically punish men for trying to be involved fathers, serves to divide women from men. We then observe that the media elevates the independent woman at the same time it disparages the involved father. Women, always more susceptible to social trends than men, especially when more educated which should be a positive social goal, internalize these conflicts and choose instead of following natural instincts toward motherhood to devote their lives to competition with men, where their productive labor is then able to be used to subsidize their own diminution of influence, genetics, and the lost opportunity to have a family. It's not commonly shared, but there are swathes of literature from women who emerged from the 1970's now lamenting their loss, long after their window for reproduction has passed, but in sadness from one side and bitterness from both men and women.

We see the institution of marriage itself degraded. There are several different historical standards one could use for marriage. One is as an economic relationship between two families, from which the dowry once existed, and which has echoes today in the symbolic although ridiculously ornate bridal ceremonies, whereby the wife's family gave resources to help support the resultant children which would bond two families in mutual support through blood and gold. That definition was surprisingly resilient, and despite its disfavor today, few issues are more destructive to a couple than financial difficulties, many of which are overcome only with the help of other family members as is natural and useful to all: a microcosm of nationalism at work.

This definition was supplanted with a view of marriage as either a bond or sacrament for those who hold faith, binding a man and woman together in perpetual unity, and understanding the purpose of this bond was partially as a celebration of love and commitment, but from the social perspective, to convey benefit and purpose to the goal of having children. The state once sought to protect and enshrine the family, understanding this institution has been the most successful social mechanism in human history. The family is the mechanism through which liberty is realized, and the inherently intrusive role of the state in individual lives is not just restrained but even opposed. Given that Leftism is the belief the state exists to take control and mandate equality, is it any surprise therefore that they have decided to try to destroy marriage by making it all things to all people, a perversion of the very intent which it tries to protect?

I have no personal animus against gays or lesbians. I think transgenderism is a mental disease and should be treated as such, with those people removed far from their ability to impact children. But, the relationships they have, as loving and caring as they may well be, are not marriage and we should no longer pretend such. The desirable relationship upon which society must be built to sustain itself, as a matter of natural dictate, is a man and woman coupling to have offspring. In as much as the state exists to ensure the future existence of the nation, the state should clearly and unequivocally state that marriage is between a man and a woman. Recognizing the value that having influence from both of the only two genders has for a child's well-being, adoption and support must be restricted to traditional marriage.

It wasn't so long ago that this was the national position. Gays basically claimed they only wanted tolerance and the ability to practice their prerogative absent threats of violence or persecution. Such a compromise struck most as fair, and even people with moral misgivings agreed to such. But the funny thing, as is always case with indulging Leftists socially, is that upon getting what they want, they take more. Tolerance became civil unions became marriages became pride parades with adults parading half naked down streets in the sight of children. Now we have transgenderism and pedophilia petitioning for acceptance also, at the same time we have bakers going to jail for refusing to bake wedding cakes for these people. Tolerance must have clearly circumscribed limits, or it fails.

The Right has been afraid to push back for fear of seeming judgmental, but if we are to refocus our nation in support of our families, we must. The good news is most of you reading this already agree with what I've written, but probably were trying not to offend by previously avoiding contemplation of this as policy. It should be, and it must be, because for family planning to work – which it must to prevent our demographic collapse – we must encourage children to be born to traditional families and discourage children being born out of wedlock. We must stop subsidizing children to people who are net consumers and provide relief to those who are net producers. Government can do much here to help, but it hasn't. That's because we've shied away from having these social fights because we have fundamentally accepted the Left's paradigm of radical equality. The price has been a reduction in the quality of the lives our children now lead, a situation for which Americans should all be deeply embarrassed.

Leftists know how to use guilt and intimidation to make us forgo our reason and pervert our very natures to satisfy their never-ending demands. Learn how to stop doing this, and we will quickly discover their power is far less than it currently seems. Let's close this chapter by considering a very different way to ethically deal with the problem of unwanted children, consonant with principles of moral respect for the children and which avoids abortion as a solution, a hateful practice which some support on utilitarian grounds, but which reduces our moral level.

If instead of offering single mothers money to have children as we do, we used a mere fraction of that money to offer access to permanent birth control, we could save hundreds of thousands of dollars, avoid the nastiness of abortions, and also ensure unwanted children are not born. I would go so far as to offer government subsidy on a strictly voluntary basis for any who wish to sterilize themselves, male and female alike, so people who choose self-indulgent lives will only be accountable for themselves and not for bringing new life into this world absent the support it needs and deserves. Having taken these steps to prevent children being born outside wedlock and absent two parents, we could ethically remove the subsidy for these children which would end the inducement and pressure encouraging the people least capable of raising children to have them.

What would we do with the massive savings? We could instead offer tax support for parents having children who are married, making clear as an unambiguous statement that we want people who are together as couples to be having the majority of our children. Not only would the children see benefits, but marriage would become more important and couples would have a stronger incentive to have deeper and more resilient relationships. We could even offer fertility support for those married couples who want to have children but struggle. All of this would be done on a color-blind basis, and it would help those families across all ethnic groups trying to live the right way, while not unduly constraining those who choose a different path.

These actions are already happening in Europe. Russia has reversed its demographic collapse. Hungary and Poland are following similar paths. Pro-natalist policies are an investment in the future, and nothing makes for better citizens than having more parents, because the very act of having a child suggests a commitment to the future and a wider perspective than one's own momentary interest. These are trends we must encourage.

We should recognize, as in so many other areas, that family planning is one place where we have – again through our inaction – ceded control to the Left. Their insanity is hurting our relationships and hurting our kids. If we don't stop them now, mandatory gender reassignments might very well be the next step. So, pushing back in favor of clear standards rooted in heritage and nature is both healthy and humane. And it would be far more popular than people imagine, because it's what most of us already cannot help but want.

Chapter 11: Culture and Education – Too Important to Ignore

Some chapters are just harder to write. There are areas where the problems are obvious, and the solutions are simple, such as immigration where we just need to keep out people who don't belong, or family planning, where we need to support families who should have children in doing so. But as we all appreciate, not all problems are so simple to address and yet sometimes, these areas matter the most. We find ourselves in such a situation with culture and education.

If you'll recall the earlier chapter on values, much energy was devoted to discussing the distinction between transactional and non-transactional values, and how what a people choose as the latter category largely distinguish civilizations and nations from one another. For both achievement as well as stability, such values need to be largely universal within a nation to ensure the collaboration and cooperation that are the core components to good order, shared aspirations, and the resultant unity that bolsters the nation. When considering which values fell into the non-transactional category, the two which keep coming to my mind are culture and education. They are also very much interlinked, but to simplify this conversation here from the beginning, let's just presume education largely shapes culture as the nature of the relationship, even as we all know culture then adjusts educational motivations.

One of the core positions of the Right which is commonly held and very much supported is that parents know what is best for their children, and as an extension of this, maximal power to determine what schools teach should be reserved to local control. More than any other issue, people relocate and argue over taxation to ensure their children receive an education that is of the highest standard, and ideally within the moral framework they want for their children. Even though public education is compulsory, we see families spend thousands to ensure their children avoid such schools in many cases because of discomfort with the offerings, or a desire to provide optimal opportunity to their offspring.

I begrudge no parent these actions. But in watching how people constantly move and shift their children, I believe this reveals how badly the education system is broken at all levels, especially within the public sector. This problem is so big, so vital, and so damaging, that we do a disservice by refusing to look at the problem from a national level. This question is what spawned "No Child Left Behind," which had a very good idea in raising standards rather than the long descent we still ride toward social promotion and the creep of relativism, but whose methodology in relying upon testing to measure achievement was far too reductionist.

Since then, the introduction of Common Core, another effort to harmonize standards, has proven an even larger calamity. If you spend the time to look at what is taught, education has been simplified to provide better results for the institutions to report at the cost of making our children less capable, more simplistic, and pushing a shared propaganda which should upset you, if you aren't already aware. I had my own unfortunate encounter with these ideas in seeing my niece's homework assignment where a second grader was taught to solve math problems using such a convoluted form of estimation that even with my fancy degree, it took me thirty minutes to make sense of it, and another hour to regain my composure after determining how asinine this approach to math really is. Common Core seems to want to make education idiot proof by reducing the capacity of the child for failure by taking challenges away from education. Like so much else in our culture, there are now prepackaged solutions to deliver predetermined outcomes.

We should oppose this, and many politicians do, but in a way which is disturbingly ineffective. States and school boards alike pass resolutions which ban Common Core, and then buy textbooks from the manufacturers who adhere to that same standard. Parents think the problem is resolved, but as the Left continues to control the media, most publishing houses, and educational curriculum through friendly unions, so many children going to public schools with better intent functionally end up learning the same garbage curriculum. I understand why so many parents, wisely in my opinion, seek out alternative schools such as Christian schools, charter schools, or resort to home schooling.

The situation gets worse at college, where basically there is an ideological litmus test where those Right of center can't get tenure and never get published. The best schools get the most slanted professors and the echo chamber from which the next generation of cultural voices emerges awash in Marxist rhetoric and subsidized by American taxpayers to express their hatred and discomfort with our country and our people. It's a dismal and terrible situation, to which our only response so far has been to advocate that control should be more localized.

A core belief of mine is that we're working on a very short time frame before the American collapse happens due to the combination of demographic replacement and ideological indoctrination. It's the one theme across all my writings, and if you take nothing else from all I write, remember that as we try to solve problems, the Left continues to gather numbers to their cause of equality through destruction. We can already see how their mob mentality is growing and the hints of violence in the future, spawned through these universities which are the beating heart of their propaganda machine, with their tendrils reaching into our most impressionable young minds.

Such concerns are why I believe we must deeply consider a national approach to our educational issues. While having parents deeply involved with education is a necessity for success, the reality is that our parents largely don't have the context or information to ensure even well-intended schools are achieving the desired results, and we have the absolute certainty under the current situation that most primary education and almost all secondary education exists to teach hatred of America as it is and as it was as the fulfillment of the ultimate Marxist plan to seize control.

With will and vision, we could enforce an alternative that would be healthier. A starting point would be to teach civics once more, with a basic understanding of the American government, and to ensure history is no longer taught as a series of misdeeds, but rather with pride for the struggles and achievements of our ancestors. We should even require our children to be able to pass the same citizenship test which non-natives must attain to demonstrate their knowledge of America and our government, so that every child who grows up and votes can do so with at least the basic ability to discern what options are offered in light of how government was designed to operate and the core values upon which America was founded.

A standardized curriculum built upon excellence, innovation, critical inquiry, and love of nation would be a source of unity. Fellowship is built upon common language, common concepts, and common experiences, and the diversity of options we have in schooling are only adding to the multicultural mess. When an inner-city school chooses to treat Ebonics as a genuine language, they facilitate the isolation that makes the politics of resentment so effective, yet if we take the position that local control of curriculum is an absolute, we play into this game whereby we again sacrifice our unity to our individuality. Should we continue to do this through our formative years, how can we expect future generations to find a way to unite us, except through the solutions proposed by their college professors wherein we must destroy all, as it does not work for anyone?

We can't simply say these problems are large and we aren't prepared to handle them when there is an alternative on the table. We need to get into the weeds of curriculum, and ensure American students are learning to love America, past, present, and future, or we will not survive much longer. We need to look at the textbooks being published and have a national conversation about standards. Those should be universal, in at least some key areas, while local control remains in other areas to reflect the geographic differences and unique needs of local areas. Such discussions will likely be highly confrontational, but we can't run from these hard conversations.

If we don't rein in our colleges, we will never regain our culture. This problem is even harder because we value freedom of speech as a core principle, an important value of our civilization and our first national priority. America without free speech would literally no longer be America. Yet, we should realize our universities have been hijacked by people who have gamed our system to turn our children against us. The more one understands this process, the more brilliant its cynicism reveals itself to be.

We pay for the privilege to send our children to universities, thinking these institutions open doors to success later in life and the professional knowledge to succeed in a field, which may or may not prove true, offering exorbitant sums to ensure our children attend. While the government subsidizes these loans at a low rate, to appear to help the children and their supportive families defray these costs, the reality is that in subsidizing education, government has caused the cost to skyrocket where increases in tuition far outpace inflation. Put in real terms one could get an Ivy League education for a few thousand dollars and a summer job if one met the standards a half century ago, where now the cost will be ten to twenty years of earnings potential, going largely to high finance which works in cooperation with the schools to consistently charge more and make more, all the while teaching hatred of America as the common denominator. It's so bad now that students who find themselves unable to make use of the useless degrees that so many earn are no longer able to file bankruptcy, a unique classification among all loans, designed only to make wealthy people wealthier, strengthen the schools at the cost of the students, and force compliance from the graduates with the agenda which stems outward from the colleges to society in general.

We see political correctness now evolving into censorship based on community standards, and that colleges which once spoke so passionately in defense of the debate of ideas to advance our civilization and increase our knowledge now passively encourage safe spaces and allow students to choose their own grades, so long as they don't offend anyone else or threaten the Leftist agenda. We see new graduates go to Silicon Valley and pervert social media into echo chambers, to Washington to open more borders, and to newspapers to preach the Gospel of how standards are dead, reason is unreasonable, and our nature is subject to their choice.

That the Left controls the universities and so influences primary education is why we, as Americans, functionally don't control our own culture. This crisis is the heart of our struggle and why we are forced now, because of inaction or lack of awareness before, to contemplate using government in ways which feel unnatural. Because our choices are incredibly constrained, and as my first volume covered in depth, the Left and those who embody their core created this situation through decades of effort, consolidation, and relentless and even selfless drive to take control of all the levers shaping how we look at ourselves in society.

How do we oppose this? We cannot simply state government shouldn't do this unless we achieve our own unitary hold on government. I've argued specifically in favor of that in multiple places as one potential solution, as this constant move back and forth between ideological extremes is unsustainable, and the Left, even if they wished, is institutionally incapable of coming back from where their embrace of resentment and identity politics has taken them...and taken us. This ground will have to be fought, and while we can preserve our idea that character matters as well as identity, we can only do that if we use government more effectively than they have, or if we unmake the means by which they force conformity.

We need to help our students at the same time we weaken our schools. Not in terms of their ability to explore new ideas or develop thought leaders, but in how they have so much money and ideological unity. Just as President Trump talks about draining the swamp, there is much we can ethically do to drain educational endowments. If the government stopped guaranteeing student loans, allowed for student bankruptcy, and offered different contingencies upon grants being offered to sustain schools, much could be done to reduce the cost of education and deplete these war chests these Leftist lobbies now hold.

Sixty years ago, the Left attacked the Churches in America by putting their nonprofit status at risk for speaking about political matters from the pulpit, silencing many moral voices for fear of financial punishment. Some of you will surely note as well that while you rarely heard political voices from ministry from the Right up until recently, the

Left often had ministers speaking their Gospel as they knew the Right wouldn't enforce such an odious and anti-free speech law against the faithful, but when they had control over the government and the IRS, they gleefully attacked our civil institutions to push the culture ever toward them. It's time for us to get tough with the schools the same way they did with the churches.

Universities largely hold their land exempt from many different types of taxation. The gains on their endowments are also tax exempt. This can and should change. We have a choice as to whether we use these as carrots to bring ideological diversity back into the mix, or whether to directly try to disable these schools from processing our youth into our adversaries. Importantly, please note that I am not advocating that their ideas should be banned from public discourse. That is against our beliefs and our faith in reason through open discourse to build a better tomorrow, but it means they no longer get to shut us down because they're offended.

The offensive we desperately need begins in the colleges, but extends to the media, where we will continue to call out fake news, and recognize the reality that six corporations now control over 90% of the media to promote a single, Leftist, globalist message. America once limited foreign control over our media, requiring local publications to be held by local owners, and we can do so once more to stop the propaganda. We can ensure that social media and the new technology-driven forms of discourse allow free speech, and bring antitrust and corruption investigations against those corporations and actors who try to constrain us from being heard. Twitter, Facebook, Google, and Apple are all prime targets, and if we don't regulate them away from silencing us now, we may not have the platform to advocate doing so later.

As nationalists and populists, we can and should consider these actions, remembering that to sustain our country, we need a common culture and an education system compatible with building and maintaining that unity. We need to recognize and honestly name those who prevent us from having the honest discussions, and as President Trump has begun with devastating effect, continue the war on political correctness, and take away any authority – real or imagined – from the gatekeepers whose very existence runs contrary to our most celebrated traditions.

Our solutions may not be perfect and there is much discussion to be had on the details of how to intervene and where, but we can be absolutely certain that whatever we come up with as alternatives to Marxist propaganda will be far better for our nation and for our children, which is the responsibility which we must always hold in the highest regard and upon which our continued existence as America must inevitably rely.

Chapter 12: Foreign Disentanglement Guarantees Independence

The next three chapters shift from protection of our culture to preserving our independence, but what's particularly interesting in reviewing how our culture operates is just how many foreign influences buy their way into American relevance. This sordid reality helps explain not just the success of globalism, but also the widespread corruption in our government and private sectors, by which the Deep State sustains itself and why those folks tend to lean Left more often than not. But it also highlights another key point of the post-Trump future, which is that we must realize that no amount of economic growth or development alone will save America in the absence of cultural unity, which can only come from a clear articulation of our values and ensuring both our government and our elites work for America First.

Indulge me a brief digression. I was walking with a friend through Portland, Maine, a very nice and mostly clean city in my adopted home state, when I had an epiphany about what was driving so much of the social conflict beyond the institutional actors and the cultural games. Cities now exist, in this global economy, much more apart from the country that surrounds and sustains them. Although through aesthetics, architecture, and custom, they often pay homage to the still existing links between what is produced around them and what they distribute, we now have a transcendent urban class who exists purely as creatures of cities, as comfortable in one city as the next, and more comfortable in a foreign city than a small town of their native homeland. Walking through the biggest city in Maine and seeing the ideas and styles expressed there, I couldn't help but admit these people live in a different world than a humble country boy like myself.

But it made an idea within my mind snap together: why do our elites no longer work for the benefit of the nation, and instead seem to despise those of us who live in flyover country who provide the food, resources, logistics, and security that enable their lifestyles? The answer must be that the leadership, now committed to a global Leftist ideology, sees themselves as a class apart, and only tolerate those of us who have traditional values and still pay homage to our nations, including our beloved America, as holdouts to an obsolete ideal. They seem to believe their world of ideas, information, and fantasy is the real one just because it is the most cutting edge, and should we annoy their thoughts with inconvenient reality, they assume what we provide can simply be replaced. How cynical are these globalists in how they exploit poor labor in backward countries to enjoy their comforts, all the while lecturing us who happen to reside in proximity to them about our habits? It's hard not to hate such hypocrisy, but I have to remind myself that people often don't think very deeply.

My story aside, the reason for this little narrative is that if America is going to continue our recovery post-Trump, we need leadership whose commitment is clearly and unequivocally to our nation and our people, not to some imagined global agenda. We need elites who see the betterment of those who suffer in this country as their singular concern, and who devote their aims to our shared satisfaction before investing us again in either these humanitarian wars which only end up hurting everyone or their various pet causes whereby we surrender our precious sovereignty to the control of others.

The Left loves pulling that trick of international legitimacy because it plays to their strength. They build up and bolster voluntary institutions to bring people together on common socialist causes, slowly assuming mandatory authority and then using their position of media dominance and ownership of high finance to cajole or coerce nations into compliance. No one ever voted for the UN to make treaties that have authority worldwide, yet in this supposedly democratic world, most accept the legitimacy of such without any questions.

Since we opened by talking about immigration, consider how their position on refugees dovetails perfectly. Signatories to a United Nations treaty on refugees agree to take whomever is given, without any ability to discern their intentions, values, or motives, and whose people may fundamentally change the culture of their new host nation. As stated earlier, up until 2018, the United States was a member of this treaty and took in more refugees than any other nation. This immigration was not widely talked about but represented hundreds of thousands of people dumped into unsuspecting communities, often against and above the objections of the local population. This perversion of the rule of law against popular sovereignty represents the worst sort of international institutionalism, a crisis that hurts America and is destroying Europe.

The United Nations does us no favors, and like many others on the Right, I believe we should leave this corrupt body. While having an international forum where diplomats can discuss matters of state has inherent value, the UN has zero right to assert almost any of the authority it claims, and should great powers ever come to conflict again, such an entity will prove as useless as the League of Nations, its immediate predecessor also proved. We don't need human rights advice from Arab nations and we don't need China checking our military aspirations. The whole thing is an expensive and unseemly farce which should be considered unconstitutional.

Like President Trump, we should be skeptics of transnational and multilateral arrangements designed to bind America's potential and growth. For so many years, we submitted voluntarily to these bonds for the false promises of a more peaceful world, of greater prosperity for our people, and that the world would show their appreciation for our leadership by adopting our values and customs. While there have been some successes, there have been far more failures as conflicts continue the same as before, and trade deals served to destroy the industrial and manufacturing economy and stagnate wage growth for over four decades. And we see rising powers like China build their countries anew on American money taken due to poor trade practices.

Our elites think this is great and this is preferable because their loyalty, by and large, is neither to America nor its people, because they are not nationalists. The Left hopes to realize the ultimate equality of a single global state under their control through these sorts of maneuvers. But we should also admit that up until recently, and still among many quarters, many of those on the Right bought into the false doctrine that free trade is always in the American interest. As Trump rightly notes, fair trade is what we need, where we develop relationships of equitable exchange, rather than hollowing out the center of our nation. This hollowing out through trade deals, as those who dogmatically take the radical free trade libertarian approach instead advocate, has been both an economic calamity for millions of our families as well as a potential national security liability. For too long, we put ideas first instead of our people first, and making a deal where we hurt our own to make a buck has been the worst and most self-defeating tendency of the Right.

We began winning when we drew the contrast and defined ourselves as the people who believe America is exceptional and sovereign and worked to promote those values unapologetically and peacefully in all our relationships, with long-time friends and one-time foes. We told allies they could no longer mooch off our misguided idealism and earned respect without losing amity. If some of these countries take greater accountability for themselves, such as we see with both Asian and European allies doing with trade and self-defense, we should reckon these developments as positive, as those are expenses the American people will no longer be required to handle alone. Replacing profit-taking with partnerships, on a bilateral basis, helps make America more prosperous and gives a foundation to ensure we protect our industries and our economic capacity moving into the future.

When it comes to outside threats, the combination of firmness and respect in recognition of national sovereignty also shifts us from the misplaced idealism that has cost many American lives and much American treasure to a foundation for peace despite disagreements. For decades, politicians have claimed that America is no longer the world's policeman, and then rushed to the answer of far too many calls revealing this intention as hollow. Even now, during Trump's regime, we remain engaged in Syria, in Afghanistan, and other places where the American people overwhelmingly desire us to draw down operations and leave. Not capriciously, but to recognize the world is going to have problems and awful places, and that America does best to not poke those beehives.

In leaving these entanglements alone, we follow the advice of George Washington and the brilliant formulation by James Monroe who restricted our involvement internationally to our hemisphere, recognizing how blessed we are by geography, and having the realistic position that the conflicts of the Old World are cyclical and perpetual, and that to engage in those abroad will only invite the worst of consequences to rebound upon us here. Terrorism is one such result, and if we ask bluntly what we've gained for what we spent, who but the globalists can pretend America has come out to the positive for our earnest efforts?

What applies to trade applies equally to defense. We find ourselves caught in so many treaties where we have volunteered to defend huge sections of the world against regional or global conflicts, and we must now ask whether this serves the strategic interest of Americans here at home.

Those who support these actions argue they sustain peace which otherwise will fail in light of external ambitions, but if we remember that war is expensive and uncertain, such doomsday predictions that the war of all against all will result should America refocus our efforts more locally and only with key select allies are overwrought. In truth, careful study of both the First and Second World War both indicate it was the existence of too many and sometimes contradictory alliances that made what might have been relatively minor conflicts into great global contests.

We pass over the inconvenient reality that both of these wars, not to mention countless others, might have proven unnecessary had these treaties not existed. We also forget Americans, by and large, did not want to enter either war, and only did so after years of agitation from the media and politicians about the dire results of waiting if we were to sit out these fights. We justify such actions by claiming these wars were utterly necessary to create the world we enjoy today, but when we look at what internationalist globalism has evolved into, I cannot help but question whether these battles were the right ones to pick. I realize that is heresy, and a position one is not allowed to take about the past, so we'll leave that aside other than to say all of us probably want to forestall the wars of the future, which would prove equally sacrosanct after the fact.

Count me as skeptical about NATO for these very reasons. Implementing a containment strategy for Russia which is nationalist and no longer communist seems obsolete, an alliance driven as much by habit as by the resentment of the Left. The Left is resentful over the reality that the Russian people finally divested themselves of the Soviet yoke and sought a path forward through national renewal, a revitalized Orthodox faith, and seeking respect for their sovereignty. What Russia has done sounds a bit like what we're trying to do here. Other than those Leftists trying to hide their own misdeeds with our uranium supply, I cannot help but think the Left tries so hard to force us to disengage with Russia for fear that by engaging with them, together we might threaten their corrupt European Union by which they are unmaking the great nations from which so many of us have our own heritage. Amity with Russia, not NATO expansion, is the key to peace in Europe and is entirely acceptable to people who place America first.

The lie told is that nationalists seek war, but the reality is nationalism is probably the world's best vehicle for peace because it recognizes that different cultures can have different spaces to pursue their own national destiny. With sound natural borders, such as we are blessed to enjoy with two oceans – hopefully soon to be supplemented by a beautiful wall to our South – we already enjoy all the space we need. If we commit to seeing America built to its fullest potential, how successful could we be?

America needs to stop putting itself up for sale, and we on the Right must lead this charge because so many of our compatriots tricked us into supporting this harmful agenda. We need to stop permitting foreign powers to lobby our government, to purchase influence, and to treat our brave military as mercenaries for their cause. Israel does this. Saudi Arabia does this. South Korea does this. Germany does this. Our men and women deserve so much better, and whatever one thinks of any or each of these countries, our core conviction should be incredibly simple: Our people exist to defend and benefit our nation and should no longer be the rent-an-army for any other nation or international institution.

What applies to defense applies just as strongly to trade, government appropriations, and our absurd practice of spending billions on foreign aid. We need to stop allowing foreign actors to buy Congress or key lobbies, and we need to take all foreign money out of our government with the strictest of regulations and penalties. As someone who worked for years in government purchasing, I remain astounded at how foreign powers could literally buy their way onto approval lists where their state subsidized industries were allowed to compete on an equal level with privately held American businesses. So many jobs have been lost through this disgusting practice, and no one even knows or seems to care because the way money moves gets lost in the unreadable morass of appropriations where billions of dollars exchange hands. How about we return to the standard where if something can be built in America, that's where our government will get their goods or services?

We can apply these same principles to the media, to propaganda, and to numerous other areas of life where if foreign powers try to cause division, we can stop them. The Left, after all their complaints about Russia, can hardly object to such actions although we should be even more vigorous in looking at what the Chinese are doing, in how they force American companies to build plants abroad, steal our intellectual property, and then build the same products for both domestic consumption and international distribution using stolen technology.

We can call out all sides who screw us, and work with anyone on a fair basis, if we genuinely embrace the America First ethic which Trump has rekindled. Such is consonant with the intention of the Founders, marked our strongest periods of social unity as well as economic growth, and we can already see the wisdom of his approach in the impressive economic numbers and greater opportunity. While the cultural conflict must remain the focus, nationalism inspires us to seek yet greater success. And, being a more prosperous and wealthy country, where more of our people find the dignity of work and our businesses can prosper, is a longstanding tradition the Republicans have supported, and which benefits our entire republic.

Chapter 13: Rebuilding America - Systems for Success

Candidate Trump spoke frequently about the need to improve our crumbling infrastructure, and this challenge is one we must take head on. The reality is that many of our public roads, highways, and power lines date back to the 1950's or earlier in some cases. The result has been substandard transportation, an antiquated rail system, a vulnerable power grid, and Americans spending far more time in traffic and far more money to replace tires, brakes, and struts than ever should have been necessary.

Equally important, sound infrastructure encourages economic development, just as when a new highway links two towns to encourage trade, commerce, and interaction. We live in both a physical world where pipes, lines, and roads are needed, and a virtual world, where improved pathways for information are equally vital to how people engage one another.

Let's start with the basics. Anyone who regularly drives, rides, or flies across this country and who has also visited other countries realizes we are falling behind. Compare our highway system to what you would find in Asia, the Middle East, or many places in Europe and it becomes clear we've allowed our once premier system to lapse behind. A lot of this can be blamed on our determination to invest so much money into social welfare to directly subsidize people that we don't have the funds available to invest in situations conducive to new opportunity, as infrastructure spending provides great value both to the government and to individuals and business.

Up until recently, the United States had an absurd level of regulations and environmental compliance requirements which constrained highway design. These regulations were used within States and counties to suppress the enhancement and maintenance of infrastructure in the same way in which nations are told they must forego industry, at least in the developed world, for fear of their output damaging some questionable metric. As a result, America has long found itself restrained from rebuilding our major pathways. Now, with more sensible regulations in place and the irresponsible ones removed during this administration, we can quickly design and build highways that will alleviate traffic and provide for safer and more frequent connections between our people, releasing our energy.

Another major opportunity could be to explore the creation of a Twenty-First century rail network for the United States for passengers and freight alike. While the historical inefficiency of Amtrak has soured many on the Right on this idea, we shouldn't forget it was the railroad which opened our settlement of the West. With trains that now travel upwards of 300 mph, imagine the convenience of being able to travel coast to coast in under a day without the hassles of airport security. Imagine how much businesses would benefit from having a new option, cheaper than trucking, and faster by two to three days in getting goods across America.

Even better than this, however, imagine some local rail networks where people whose careers oblige them to work in the cities could choose to live their lives in the country. The single most determining factor in how people view the world seems to be their population density, and in countering the Left's desire to consolidate all of us into more densely packed hives of humanity, we could launch a rebirth of the small town with small business and personal entrepreneurship to benefit, alleviating strain on our highways, and suffusing not just resources but partnership throughout the country.

While I'll admit the city folk can be grating at times if one has become accustomed to the country, doesn't it seem like forging organic ties that link the urban and the rural to one another must be a bigger part of national renewal if we are to find a way to depart from the current cultural collision course? Our leadership should stress how we can help our rural folk compete, but also ways to culturally ensure our ideas stop being so foreign to the people who live in our cities. The media won't do it, the schools won't do, so maybe an old-fashioned conversation will have to suffice.

Airports are a mess and our security procedures are taxing and invasive. Without sacrificing our protection, more can be done to streamline the TSA and get flying back toward being a joy instead of a hassle. The reality is that we spend a great deal of money to pay for the mere appearance of security, where any qualified analyst can show you a dozen different vulnerabilities still present in the air travel system for threats, not to mention in more harmful areas. The way to deal with those risks is to not foolishly engage in foreign adventurism but to instead have strong, clear, and powerful border security. But, the basic airport quality in the United States is also not up to par, and State and Federal partnerships should be encouraged to improve these areas.

Maybe my time as a civil servant is showing here, but two areas which don't get nearly the attention they require are our plumbing systems and our power infrastructure. Starting with the plumbing, we saw the sad episode in Flint during the Obama regime – a situation that exists in many cities and towns where Americans do not have reliable access to safe drinking water or adequate sewage facilities. Much of this is due to old lines breaking down, as is unavoidable after being stretched in many cases for decades beyond their intended use, because politicians will find money for dealing with a tragedy, but never budget the required funding for sound maintenance to prevent calamities in the first place. It's a terrible and reckless habit that is repeated all too often, and the Federal government should appropriate funds to make sure new water and sewage lines can be installed where needed, and that existing lines are properly maintained. There are many things that can be done beyond subsidy which would help immensely, which include streamlined regulations, combined purchasing, and utilizing resources like the Army Corps of Engineers to help as they do with larger projects.

Speaking of larger projects, fixing the national energy grid must be a priority. More than perhaps any other vulnerability, the electric grid represents an angle through which our whole system can be put at risk either through a natural disaster, a solar flare, or in the event of conflict or terrorism, the burst of an EMP weapon which would fry most electronics that are not hardened. It would cost money to protect against these problems, but the cost is slight in consideration of the consequences of being unprepared for an event which is likely, for recurring natural reasons, to happen within this century.

When we fix the power lines, we should think about increasing our power generation capacity. President Trump has opened the spigots on energy independence, building up our oil, natural gas, and clean coal capacities, approving multiple pipelines to transport goods, and made America into a net energy exporter for the first time in many decades. Adding Liquefied Natural Gas (LNG) terminals and refining capacity can only help and strengthen our independence, but we should see a diversified mix of energy and I hope hydroelectric power comes back on the table. Dams are incredibly effective sources of both flood control and energy generation, representing a virtually limitless source of clean power, and could prove especially helpful and efficient in getting low cost energy to rural areas. Since the Seventies, they've fallen into disfavor due to the environmental lobby, but we can and should reverse this where it makes sense, while taking the local situation and genuine environmental concerns into consideration.

As we deal with electrical lines, America could also update and upgrade its national fiber-optic network. States across this country have been investing in high speed Internet capacity to ensure even towns as small as Jackman, Maine are just a fingertip away from the national discussion and everything America has to offer. Our future development depends upon our ability to engage one another, and the power to have a newer and stronger communications network is vital to our future success.

Just as important as all the upgrades we mention herein, we need to make investment to secure our existing infrastructure which has fallen into decay and disrepair. As we remember most poignantly from the sad episode of Hurricane Katrina, the failure of the levees led to massive loss of property and human life. There are hundreds of dams, sewage systems, and power stations which operate well beyond intended capacity, and are forced to do so without any planned alternative or adequate maintenance. Such shortsightedness makes future tragedy inevitable, and we must undertake a comprehensive survey of what is broken and work quickly to fix what we are not better served to replace.

Although not strictly an infrastructure question, as part of pushing for hardware through which we can have the capacity needed for the data flows of the future, we should also clearly and boldly articulate a view of the Internet for the future. I very much opposed the decision whereby ICANN, the consortium which governs website domain names, was given over to international authority and taken away from the American control which saw the early net adopt our sacred principle of freedom of speech and association. Now that ICANN is no longer under the authority of the American government and is not beholden to the First Amendment, we see the creeping influence of totalitarianism in how censorship is being falsely presented as virtuous, and we know from our own history that only the free exchange of ideas ensures the protection of liberty and advancement of civilization. We should codify this requirement embodied in our First Amendment for those sites who wish to operate in our most lucrative market and push back against what the globalists in the EU and communists in China are trying to do by building walls around information they don't like.

What distinguishes America is that we face the unknown, challenge it, and learn from the encounter. Nationalists don't fear having our people see new ideas, because we actively seek the best ideas rather than those which provide only for the most control. We live in a dangerous time where we run a real risk of losing control over the information infrastructure for the future, and while I am certain an alternative would emerge, it's going to be better for both America and the entire world if our ways in this area exist to bring freedom – not as guns – but as ideas to the rest of the world, just as we see our nationalism now increasingly paralleled in Europe and elsewhere.

If we embrace a bold vision of a rebuilt America, pride cannot help but swell at the same time safety is increased, prosperity renewed, and opportunity encouraged. In these matters, one would hope even the Left would see value, although given how they invest in the cities which they overwhelmingly run, perhaps even that modicum of sanity is too optimistic. They seem content to have people live in hovels, like in the tent cities which have now become an increasingly disturbing feature of the California landscape, but we should not allow their intransigence and folly to prevent us from developing our nation as most Americans would want, and from which they would benefit. Let them see clean cities and healthy towns connected to one another, and then give our people the choice of the future they want. Given such options, perhaps those trapped under that hateful ideology might finally find their way forward and we should welcome those who walk away.

If the Republican Party shifts from the party of small government to the party of better government, as we nationalists should advocate, we give ourselves a wider toolbox through which we can solve the issues which impact our people. If an investment of one dollar in infrastructure will elicit many dollars in return in both business growth and the resultant tax revenue, then it makes sense, both qualitatively and quantitatively. We need to learn how to look across the public and private ledger at the same time, and to have our government help our businesses, and make sure our businesses are equally invested in our nation. Friendly trade policies and less regulation are the carrot, and the promise of tariffs are the stick in case they forget that even though businesses can and should work internationally, their presence in America must always be to the benefit of and respectful to our people. They do not own us – they serve us, and we welcome such.

The last issue worth touching on as regards infrastructure is health care. While this might seem like an odd place to conclude this chapter on infrastructure, if you think of nationalism as protecting the body of the people, then nothing is more important than ensuring that the people themselves are well, as that is how our collective health is maintained. Our Founders certainly never envisioned health care as a right, but they also didn't have access to all the life preserving and extending technologies which we now enjoy. The reality that some have access to these and some are left to die because of their economic standards should trouble us, just as clearly as the death panels which the Affordable Care Act hid behind hospices did upon the adoption of that poorly constructed law.

Hopefully, the Republicans will finally repeal this law, and replace it with a solution to make health care affordable and accessible. The economics of this will be complex, but the solution needs to ensure that patients and doctors make decisions regarding care together, voluntarily, and that costs are controlled intelligently so that we don't pay more than foreign countries do, as currently happens with prescription drugs, but also be sure not to stifle innovation. Patients should have more options, with better quality, and less cost, and the government will have to step in at times to provide support, as it does currently with Medicare, but perhaps more efficiently.

There's a ton that could be done which would only streamline how medicine works. The arcane coding rules alone in ObamaCare cost a great deal in administrative overhead, as well as not having caps on medical malpractice which allows the malpractice insurance racket to continue adding costs. While I'm not against anyone making money for providing a professional service, the reality is that big pharmaceutical companies and big insurance companies work in tandem to design legislation like this wherein the emphasis is on treatment rather than cures, and profitability rather than health. That's a disgrace, and one where we as those who care for our people should be most vocal.

From these understandings, I'm confident a better system can be designed. It will have both private and public elements with choice paramount and costs constrained, especially when it comes to non-essential items. There is no perfect answer to this, but a Republican Party which follows the trail set by President Trump in saying we will care for our citizens will only be that much stronger in proving the Left's common complaint we are heartless as a lie.

Chapter 14: Finance – Take Back Our Money

In seeking our independence to fulfill this nationalist vision, we must conclude in that area which might prove most essential: Finance. The reality is that money makes the world go around, and the behaviors we see from Wall Street play such a decisive role in shaping culture and our economics that to ignore their influence would make the rest of this inquiry trivial. Not only do the financiers run this country and own much of our government via their political contributions and the networking they offer, but they're also the heart of the globalist project which we must confront if we are to be run by We, the people, instead of They, the powerful.

Allow me to tell just a little bit about my own political, philosophical, and ideological evolution which might help this whole chapter and topic make much more sense. I repeat some version of this story in each book I write, not because my previous articulations were inadequate, but because there is a series of events and facts which people reading my writing must understand to make sense of America, nationalism, and why things are the way they are.

I came up through the libertarian mindset although I have been a social conservative for as long as I could remember. My basic orientation, like many young people of my generation, was to adopt a live and let live approach, and so I shied away from trying to impose my views as any good Republican then did, instead arguing that we should just speak our views, reach who we could, and allow the others to exist as they chose. There was a time not so long ago when that seemed far less crazy than it seems today, but I guess that's because so many of us never understood how far the Left was ready to go to feed the mob.

Anyway, I had done some minor work for different political campaigns and candidacies, but my first major involvement was for the Ron Paul campaign in 2008. Looking back, the grassroots effort made then was a great time for everyone involved, had tons of interesting people, and was ahead of its time in having key elements of the later Tea Party and Trump nationalist efforts. The idea that we should have restrained foreign policy to protect our liberties is a timeless American and frankly, Republican value, one which neoconservative thinkers usurped. Finding a better articulation in peace through strength as Trump likes to say, the thread between what we did then, and what he does now is instead of looking for war to remake the world, the idea was to put America first out of respect for both our people and others. As the peace talks in North Korea indicate, the impulse was spot on, though even then I felt that a more muscular interpretation was open and useful.

The other key issue, more relevant to this chapter, was in learning how finance worked and the role of the Federal Reserve within the American system. The single greatest sell-out of this country, and the scam by which the Left can even be here was through the creation of this private bank which controls the distribution of money throughout these United States. The creation of the Federal Reserve, in tandem with the creation of a Federal income tax, fundamentally transformed America from a free and sovereign nation with limited government and which had control over its nation to a client state beholden to private economic actors and interests at home and abroad. Strong words to be certain, but if you understand both what the Fed is and how money really works, you begin to understand how the Fed is the tail that wags the American dog, and how deeply we've paid for surrendering our liberty to them.

What is a dollar? It's a piece of paper. It currently enjoys purchasing power for obtaining both goods and services. It also serves as a store of value, and a strengthening one as Trump improves our trade relationships, our balance sheet, and our economic growth. But what intrinsic value does it have beyond the paper and linen used in its construction? There was a time, not so long ago, when a dollar functioned much like a check. Those dollars issued by the United States Treasury were redeemable for silver or gold, tangible goods of perpetual value. But today's dollars are currently backed only by the full faith and credit of the United States Government. They're fiat currency.

Dollars have value because we believe they do. If you've built your life, as so many of us have at one point or another, around the reality that money governs so much of our existence and you have striven to earn dollars from another through work and effort, then the dollars mean even more to you because of what they cost you in labor and energy. But inherently, they have no more backing than the money from a Monopoly board game, no constraints on how many can be produced, and for those who put them out there, this is the key to the whole scam.

The Federal Reserve makes up money out of thin air, accountable to no one, audited by no one, and privately owned. Through the money they release or retain, they can rig the whole economy. They make up the money, charge the US Treasury and the taxpayer for the privilege, then lend it to their constituent banks for low interest or sometimes zero interest, who then in turn lend the money to businesses and individuals for profit. To get even more detailed, for every dollar a bank owns, they can basically lend ten out through fractional reserve banking on the presumption that not all account holders will ask for their money at once. If this sounds like making money out of thin air, that's precisely what it is, and that's now the foundation of not just the American, but the global economy, and why you see banks and financiers at the heart of globalism. They make up money and we spend our whole lives fighting and struggling to obtain what they simply imagine and distribute.

If you've never heard this before and your mind is blown, take heart because you're not alone. It takes years for those of us who learn this reality to recover, but it's well-documented and researched, and I'll offer recent proof of how the scam operates. When Obama was destroying our economy through excessive regulation and subsidizing both cronies and all of the special interest groups of the Left, the Federal Reserve reduced their prime rate to zero and called this quantitative easing. In English, that means the central bank gave other banks free money to sustain the economy, flooding the market with more dollars, so prices rose due to inflation even as wages stagnated. The bank basically covered for Obama, as they do with most Leftist Presidents, using their power to stimulate the economy with more fiat currency to conceal just how damaging the economic policies of the Left are to this country.

When Trump came into power and moved the country toward a sounder economic basis, lowering taxes and regulations to encourage growth, the Federal Reserve responded to these beneficial actions by raising the interest rates. Now, banks would have to pay to lend money, passing those costs directly on to consumers, retarding growth through the creation of a stronger dollar, but essentially limiting the positive influence of Trump upon the economy. That this economic renewal is succeeding despite this deliberate drag that the Fed has placed upon it proves both how terribly Obama managed the economy, but also how helpful liberating the economy and shifting our production and trade policies to a nationalist basis can be.

But the Federal Reserve remains the biggest threat to the Trump boom because they continue raising the interest rates. Conventional economics teaches this is healthy to prevent deflation, maintaining a constant rate of growth, and avoiding the cycle of boom and bust which is inherent in all human endeavor, instead building this fantasy of perpetual managed growth with imaginary money upon which global finance now rests. From this foundation, more permutations emerge as derivatives and other financial instruments which, when properly understood, are revealed as proposition bets for this imaginary market.

How does this impact us? Have you ever wondered why a person like George Soros seems to have limitless money with which to agitate Leftists hordes? I'll use an example from today as I write watching yet another caravan of migrants who supposedly are desperately poor, work their way across country after country with minimal disruption, smart phones in hand, somehow feeding and paying for themselves to invade upwards toward America to sculpt our politics and, if admitted, help shift our country further Left. The answer all comes back to the Fed.

When you understand the relationships between the Fed, the European Central Bank, the Bank of England, the Bank of International Settlements, and other related institutions, what you come to realize is these big banks make up money, make the conditions by which we can get it, and we subject our lives to their demands, putting our nations at their disposal. The only people who have ever stood against them firmly were neither the capitalists who looked only to their own personal wealth nor the communists who embraced their collectivism as useful, but rather the nationalists who demanded the right to go their own way. Heroes like Andrew Jackson who overcame an assassination attempt to keep America free and sovereign from crippling debt. Or like Benjamin Franklin, who noted that the effort to force funny money on the colonies played a key role in our American Revolution, a fact never taught in history texts and often concealed.

How Soros and people like him get their money is through ownership of the banks, which lend and loan the money they create at most advantageous terms to allies who put forth a message of globalized centralized control. They purchase the media, willing to lose money in infinite amounts – as only those with infinite money can – for the real investment in shaping our minds against love of nation, toward hatred of virtue and counter to our very selves. They use their infinite money to own the institutions where their patronage – bribes – ensure our compliance as we struggle to earn decent lives according to rules they've created for us.

Perhaps it is easier for Christians to understand just how toxic this scam is, as the love of money is the root of evil – the desire to place your will unilaterally over others without any concern for them. Like any nationalist, I believe will matters immensely, but I believe it is the will of our people beyond money and in pursuit of virtue and higher ambitions upon which we should base our efforts.

Once you understand all these things, where *Someone Has to Say It* goes into much more detail, you begin to understand why no amount of economic growth can ever beat this scam. The only way you beat someone with infinite money and the will to use it to unmake everything you love, is to instead walk away from centering your life around money, and instead invest in the social capital of people, recognizing the true nature of economics is not dollars but exchange of goods, services, and ideas between people in the hope of achieving a better future individually and together. You rebuild your nation.

As nationalists, we should directly go after the banks that work against our interest, and we can begin this as Republicans by taking up the first task of auditing the Federal Reserve. What distinguishes us from our opponents is our requirement that justice be served, and we should examine all their holdings, see who they helped and what decisions they made, and make clear as a matter of public record beyond any doubt who owns these banks. Even as

Congress enjoys the clear constitutional authority for such an inquiry, people who ask questions too deeply on these matters – including some members of Congress who served in the previous century – died under suspicious circumstances.

As you go more deeply down some of these rabbit holes around which our reality is constructed, you find that the battle between Left and Right, the fight between their equality of death and our quality of life, and wars with darker parallels where the stakes get higher, and the battles become more vicious. We're permitted to have certain arguments and discussions regarding policy and programs. But if you speak about identity and demography, you might find yourself ostracized and on a hate list. If you speak about how banks run the world with their funny money, set against the labor of honest people trying to do the right thing but so often serving the system which holds them in bondage, all that might be left of you are some forbidden words people are punished to even read.

It takes courage to combat this. I believe in transparency, and I believe we should name names of the people, institutions, and their origins who run this system. Look beyond George Soros and look at the patterns of who runs finance, who benefits, and what they do. They are Leftists, they are communists, they are globalists, but what else is there? Who are they? Where did they come from? What are their values and beliefs? Find those answers and you've found why America First has been stopped every time it has started, as has been the case with every sovereign nation in the West that went down this path.

I have my own beliefs about what happened, but that's not what matters. What matters is that you learn to ask these questions, and as you do, what you may discover is that what matters most is having people beside you whom you can trust, and with whom you can work to build the America you want together. Reality, in its simplest form, is the collective expression about all our choices about what we want to be, in accordance with our nature, governed by reason, and bolstered by faith. I place my faith in Americans, not in money.

That's why I close my list of policies and ideas about how we make sure we Make America Great Again by sharing with you exactly whom we need to stop if we hope to get to the root cause of this Leftist globalist inhumane subversion. My hope is that this framework has given you mental tools for the struggle ahead, because I regret to inform you that it only gets harder going forward, and there are no constraints in what our enemies will do and whom they will use to oppose us. We've seen the swamp, but to penetrate it and drain it means going to dark places like where the all-seeing eye rests upon all of us, as it does for the almighty dollar.

Should we audit the Fed, we will end the Fed. When we do that, we can fix our finances, constrain the banks that finance our enemies and our bondage, and liberate our people and the world to choose a new path. The economy won't collapse but will instead be stronger as the US Treasury resumes its Constitutional role in producing our currency, and we will not find ourselves so burdened by debt and malign influence. That's how America was honestly built and must be at the heart of how we, as nationalists, see it restored.

Knowing these challenges, the issues that matter to our people, and how our nation is restrained from reaching its fullest potential, let's now think about how we might take what we've learned, and how we can utilize this unique opportunity which Donald Trump has bravely forced open, to save our beloved America.

Chapter 15: Next Steps

There's a major difference between knowing what must be done and understanding how to go about achieving our goals. But if we want to make America First more than a campaign slogan from President Trump, and instead the future that our children live one hundred years from now, what's needed is an intelligent and thoughtful plan designed to ensure the changes we're making now and continue making into the future survive and have time to bear the rich fruit we know they will.

It's an unfortunate tendency in political activism to create many more agendas and platforms than people will read or could ever enact, most of which are based on either an idealistic restatement of principles or unrealistic goals and objectives. Such detail, although useful for thinking and organizing, is the equivalent of telegraphing the entire plan to the hateful Left, and because we want to keep winning, this book does not go into that levels of detail. If you want to get into those weeds, follow me at http://www.nationalright.us where we figure out how to ensure the Right is run by the Nationalists, and where we deliberately exist as allies to but outside the institutional parties and lobbies so we can do what must be done.

But for our goals, we're going to set five simple guidelines we need to meet to save America. These are broad enough that all people of good character will be welcome and can contribute but serve as the guideposts that will lead us forward without any mistake.

Step 1: Re-Elect President Trump in 2020

President Trump is an exceptional leader whose vision to restore this country's pride has stirred the hearts of millions of our fellow countrymen and whose policy talents are exceeded only by his ability to control and provoke the media. Trump forces the Left to reveal themselves, showing how dark their agenda will be if implemented, and the hypocrisy by which they elevate the least helpful while attacking the most productive. More than any articulation of philosophy on the Right, what will awaken our fellow patriots to the threat they pose against our success in the future, is seeing the Left firsthand make clear what they intend.

At the time of this writing, my hope is the Republican Party is wise enough not to support any major opposition during the 2020 Primary season, although it would not surprise me in the least if some corporate establishment type runs a lackluster though unsurprisingly well-funded campaign to unseat our President. The donor class, who lived very well-off free trade policies, has profound misgivings about putting the welfare of Americans above their own personal enrichment. They will want to return to the days before tariffs and re-negotiated trade agreements leveled the playing field for working Americans and our small business owners alike.

Another key benefit to Trump being in office from a strictly political perspective is that while he serves, being a conservative or nationalist will not make you automatically a prospective terrorist or threat to the State in the eyes of law enforcement. For as many complaints as we should have about the current inefficacy of the Justice Department in going after the wrong people, a matter which the President must solve here in the latter two years of his first term, what is equally true is we don't have the DOJ funding criminals in inner cities as part of community policing guidelines as they did under Holder and coming after people like the Tea Party who only advocated for following the rule of law in adherence to the Constitution.

What we have in President Trump is the chance to demonstrate that the narrative that nationalism is a violent and hateful philosophy is just another lie put out by the Left and parroted by their cohorts in the fake news media. Considering how we know both the media and the Left, two players on the same team as they have been for a very long time, both hate nationalism, doesn't that suggest to you that therefore nationalism might be the exact vehicle best suited to protect our traditional beliefs and practices, the rule of law, and pride in our country and our people? You don't have to be as far Right-wing as I am to see the truth in that statement, and to understand also this reality: That which damages our enemies, strengthens our position and our resolve.

The best news is that while we will set ourselves up well for the political struggles ahead, as a beaten Left will certainly be a dangerous adversary, all Americans will benefit under better policy. Peace is far more likely than war, as we work to draw down the conflict in Korea and put Asian politics on a realistic footing. China's trade imbalances and technical theft will finally be confronted, something we know the Left will never do, despite all their claims to love the working man and his industrial labor, because they love foreign communists more than American citizens.

We see this even more clearly in immigration, where hordes of Latino socialists are encouraged to run across the border and deplete our system by drawing down the welfare state at the expense to both poor Americans who legitimately need that help and draining useful resources from businesses and taxpayers who could otherwise invest in efforts intended to benefit the people of our nation. We know that the Left opposes the wall for the same reason they oppose having basic voter identification, the same standard which governs nearly every other financial or important transaction in the United States. They want illegals to come here because they know they will vote overwhelmingly for the Democrats, and these people are sadly used as a weapon to compel the rest of us into submission.

One does not have to hate the migrants to understand these facts. In truth, I do not blame them for their efforts to come to our wonderful country, despite the costly impact they've had in many places. If I were living in Venezuela, a communist hellhole that took a prosperous oil producing country and turned it into a place so dysfunctional they can no longer feed themselves, I too might migrate northward. But the consequences of their poor national decisions are their own, and while there is always room for private charity for those so moved, the obligation of America is to learn from those mistakes and avoid allowing feelings to persuade us against better judgment to keep our doors open to everyone, at dire cost to those already legally here. We have no obligations other than that, and though the media will paint such clear assertions as harsh, it is for love of our fellow citizens that we must be firm and forthright.

President Trump was elected to protect this country, and we should vote him a Congress that will finally pay to not just build the wall, but to deport all the illegals who break the law just by being here, end chain migration and reform our immigration system on a basis that benefits us. Upon making those needed preliminary reforms, it's high time that we close our doors for a while to all but those who are most like us, because as this book has made clear, we have a major cultural division we need to solve internally and giving the other side more people with which to swarm the existing majority is poor policy.

We know we will be in good hands until at least 2024 with President Trump at the wheel, and we can take the civic nationalism he has introduced and use that as the foundation for defining the Americans of the future as the very best of people with healthy values, good order, and living in both prosperity and stability.

Step 2: Ensure the GOP is the Nationalist Party

To accomplish the next step to re-elect President Trump and to ensure our leaders who follow him adhere to a compatible vision of the future, we need to work however we can to ensure the future of the Republican Party is to serve as counterpoint to the globalist vision of the Democrats by firmly and proudly embracing nationalism. There is nothing more natural for those who claim love of country than to acknowledge their first duty lies in loving the people themselves, and to recognize that not all people are blessed enough to be Americans.

Our obligation to our people is absolute but restrained in that only those citizens who live in this country, and ultimately who embrace, share, and promote our beliefs are those with whom we can build a future. While we should continue using our superior faculties of reason and appeals to our higher nature to awaken our fellow citizens from the nightmare which so many have unwittingly embraced, we need to also recognize the reality that obligations from the nation to the people also require commitments from the people in return. We need patriotism to mean more than dissent, a facile definition the Left has used to unmake our values, and instead define patriotism as including the willingness to submit oneself to a larger achievement, and the dream of a better America that is unique, exceptional, and honors its own people and glorious heritage.

Republicans have run from taking strong stances on important issues for far too long for fear of being labeled or branded by the Left in derogatory terms. But as has been revealed during these first two years of Trump's regime, even if you are as conventionally right as someone like Brett Kavanaugh, someone who probably couldn't offend if he tried, the Left is still going to consider you a racist, a bigot, a Nazi, and will label you as such. I've lived under that fire and will tell you something I learned as a very small child which can give us all strength: "Sticks and stones will break my bones, but words will never hurt me." When the Left goes after you with false accusations and slander, like they do with these patently false sexual allegations or attempts to smear the character of good men and women, stand up to them. More importantly, stand up for others who find themselves in such peril when you know these claims are false.

When we stand for one another, united on the Right by the principle of justice and fair determination, exercise of both freedom of thought and freedom of speech, we weaken their cultural conditioning and the control they impose upon us and by which our fellow countrymen are held in bondage. Stop signaling in support of their language of victimization and oppression, and instead assert that we will follow reason, nature, and virtue, wherever they may lead, and have the courage to face that greatest of frontiers, that of the mind, without the limits they place upon us about what is and is not acceptable. We can have values, but we must choose them for ourselves instead of the media or the academics.

Moreover, we must shake the Republican Party free from its reliance on donors and money which distract us from our larger duty to defend our nation and its people. We need to move away from the belief that government is always bad, which keeps us from addressing issues of real concern, and instead adopt a balanced position that remains skeptical about government, but recognizes that sometimes we must address problems at that level and have faith that our worst will still be better than their best. Most importantly, such an attitude reveals the will to invest in America and demonstrates to our people that our leadership not only possesses reason, but also shows great care toward the dreams, ambitions, and struggles of our people.

We've let the Left bludgeon us for almost a century now, and portray us as uncaring people, when it is our very concern that has served to restrain us so many times from acting against them. We've swallowed our tongues too often, when we knew what they wanted was just wrong. We didn't speak out because we wanted peace, and because we cared more about their people than they cared about us. We've seen how they think of us: Deplorable, reprehensible, toxic. And we have seen how they consider us, with emotions ranging from hatred to contempt, and how they mobilize against us with threats of violence and guarantees of intimidation. How can we meet halfway with that?

That's why we need leadership within the Republican Party that understands nationalism, and which engages and interacts to help strengthen the resolve at all levels. If you've never been involved with local politics, reach out and see how you can help. Support a candidate or support a cause, and do not be afraid to confront those who allow fear to divert them from what must be done. Vote in primaries and make sure the Republicans make the RINO into an extinct species, because we need people of character and resolve to overcome the challenges ahead.

Step 3: Reject Compromise as Policy

Too often, we are told compromise is the virtue upon which our nation must rely, but this is another lie told by the Left, and how they have stealthily undermined so many of our great institutions and beliefs. For the compromise they offer only ever goes in one direction, toward their dangerously alluring but ultimately damning belief that in absolute equality will be found the best fulfillment of our dreams and hopes. They promise everything to everyone, satisfying as many as they can by taking from those who earned more, and destroying the very will of humanity to achieve and create.

If the Right offers quality and the Left offers equality, and we meet them halfway to enjoy peace and dialogue, what are we really offering? We agree to be less than our better selves, support policies less than we know we should, and support values that are less than we really believe – all to satisfy people whose ultimate position must be to support no values at all, no morality, no responsibility, and no judgment. We surrender that which best attracts people to our cause, isolating ourselves in shock after such agreements, and wonder how the Left has won away a once more vigorous culture and civic life to this hodgepodge of multiculturalism, built upon dissent and disagreement, a rot spreading outward from our cities to corrupt the whole nation.

They promise more but deliver less. They call tolerance what is truly just indifference. They claim openness, but close their minds to any ideas but their own opinion that we must all be equal. Such absolute equality exists only in death and the despair that surrounds it. That is why I call Leftism unabashedly evil, because even though it promises man dominion over this world of clay and dust, it only destroys the spirit and that light within us, through which we overcome this hard and dangerous place. I know we're not allowed to label our opponents with more than milquetoast comments on the Right, but this must change if we are to survive.

America faces a time of choosing about who we are and what we will be. Namby-pamby articulation of our moral vision will only lead to defeat, because whatever else one might say about the Left, they are committed and fervent in their belief. As much as it disgusts us to see what they support, and as true as it is that their people are often paid for their activism, between leadership and activists alike on the Left, which is inclusive of its most fervent supporters, the willingness to engage and fight to determine the future is rising. Their will is strong even though their cause unjust, and we will see their love of identity politics, of resentment, and eventually their embrace of terror to be foisted upon us to force compliance or submission. Will we face them? Will we have sufficient strength, and will we be able to take whatever we need from whatever field we require, from the fields of thought, to the field of elections, to perhaps the ultimate contest for our very lives?

No man knows the future, but we do know that the Left is itching for a fight, and they promise that they will only stand down if we surrender to their views, and their vision of our American future. I don't think we should do that, because from everything I understand of their beliefs, that would be a be sentence worse than death for both us and all but a select few of their side as well. We have an opportunity to be so much more, a door Donald Trump kicked open with courage and valor, and through which we have a beachhead to build a beautiful future rooted in values, respect for our nation, and resolve against the false conventional wisdom.

The sooner we stop agreeing to foolish compromises, the better the outcomes will be. There will be conflict, but there is no man or woman who desires equality with those who have less. In this, there is hope for us all, because the equality we need is that of opportunity, where striving and achievement are rewarded, and for those who attempt to fly but fail, we provide a safety net and encouragement for them to lift themselves up again. They might be crawling beneath us, but we are eagles who can soar high above. And when we learn to fly, we can pick them off at our leisure as we build our nests far above their reach and comprehension. We can go places they cannot because we still have our dreams and our independence, and all they have are the grubs over which they interminably fight.

Reject compromise and embrace virtue. That is how we reclaim not just our nation but renew a civilization which has been tricked into losing faith in itself.

Step 4: Elect a Strong Nationalist in 2024

We all remember what living under President Obama was like. It was so easy to slip into that miasma of believing hope was lost and mediocrity was all we could achieve. With the government working to suppress our ambitions, and our very being so constrained by law and interventions that life itself seemed a burden, a suppression of our will to exist, we wasted eight years of our lives. Should another Democrat come to office, have no doubt they will take all our accomplishments during Trump's time and plunder the wealth we created and submerge us even more violently back into suppression.

Consider how quickly Trump has been able to undo so many of Obama's achievements, liberating us from threats like ISIS, now squelched into submission, from the gang violence and immigrant perpetrators who used to own our streets, but now face ICE and other law enforcement empowered to act for our protection. Remember how our manufacturing was once thought dead, cut off by the deadly combination of self-defeating regulations and trade deals designed to make foreign markets better for building our goods than our own. In just a few short years, and with less help from Congress than he deserved, Trump undid all Obama imposed, and now we are stronger, freer, and more optimistic than we have been in decades.

Nationalism is working, but we must not delude ourselves into thinking what Trump has given us will last forever, unless our movement works constantly to support these ideas and elect people who think this way. Of paramount importance is ensuring the Presidency always remains not just in Republican hands, but in the hands of a nationalist who understands what President Trump has begun and listens to our people and considers their needs in how we further develop and expand this excellent beginning into a deep current that brings even more members of our society into a national renewal based upon unity through vision.

This book suggests how that path must work, in how civic nationalism can be used through stronger government action to rebuild our culture along both the lines of what our people want today and our historic achievement and values. As our culture is permitted to renew, it will organically shift from government support to popular support and rebuild the bulwark against which these Marxists on the Left now have free rein. Should we rule wisely, we will crack their mirage of false equality, demonstrating through our very success a future they could not have imagined, much less create, and awaken our people to unlimited possibility. In such action, we can reunite America, and pick up where our ancestors left off, making one people out of many.

Walking this path will not be easy and will require leaders with courage and vision. Those men are out there, learning from President Trump, considering new ideas, and asking hard questions about how we get there. We need to be selective about whom we support, be honest about who supports what we want, and be unafraid to draw clear distinctions between ourselves and those who oppose us. Policy will be controversial and confrontational, but so long as it is rooted in reality rather than fantasy, we will have an advantage in that what we suggest will always work better.

I firmly believe 2024 be the single election which decides our future. After eight years of losing to President Trump, the Left will be hungry and even feral for victory. They will be ready for a fight, and absent the many advantages of incumbency, the Republicans will be vulnerable. The remnants of the Never Trump crowd and their donors will select a candidate. But we, the nationalists, who propelled Trump over seventeen other professional politicians, will need to make sure we have our candidate and that the party ultimately selects this person if we are to win. Because, we know the Trump model works, and while our next selection will almost certainly lack the irreplaceable charm and charisma of our 45th President, their ability to build upon his foundations might prove even more important in the passage of time.

Step 5: Defeat the Left and Do Not Let Them Return to Power

When Trump was elected in 2016, our country stood at the precipice of collapse. Our industry was gone, our spirit languishing, and our values were held in contempt. The Left had so demoralized us that we sat in submission, watching as their coalition of the ascendant remade our beloved home in their perverse image. We sat quietly as they destroyed our historic artifacts as glibly as the Taliban destroyed those Buddhas in Afghanistan. We shut our mouths and awaited as the silent majority for deliverance from a future we did not want but which no one seemed willing or able to stop.

Trump stopped that, and reminded us as men and women, patriots all, that America is a special place built upon opportunity and character, that our history, from Europe and our own domestic heritage alike, was neither dead nor forgotten, but merely waiting to be awakened. Now, we are awake again and coming out in huge numbers to say that our country is not going to begin a long slow descent, but instead we stand perched with the potential of full revival.

All that will change in a moment if the Left takes power. They're angry and winning the House has only made them hungrier. They were on the verge of ultimate victory and stood ready to seize complete control of our governance as fully as they had our government. They were about to use population displacement to ensure a new permanent majority in their own image, playing resentment politics to mobilize their forces, against our current majority and to usurp the country we built by perverting the very principles through which we were kind enough to allow so many outsiders to join us.

If they come to power, they will undo all Trump has done, and open the door to this country to foreign influence and foreign people to renew their push toward an unassailable permanent majority based on envy and resentment, weaponizing democracy through immigration and an inevitable amnesty to put legal polish on the invasion they allowed as the means to take control. As it is, they're only two decades from reaching this goal through existing birth rates, but how much more quickly will they get there if given unchecked power?

We must oppose them, and we must do whatever is necessary to prevent the Left from taking power back over the Executive Branch. We should also aim to deny them control over the Congress with nearly equal vigor, but while such defeat would be harmful enough, loss of the White House from here on out would not just be catastrophic, but a death sentence for the original vision of these United States.

Whatever must be done to stop this is what is needed, and each of us needs to adopt this mindset, understanding as I explained in my second book *The Coming Civil War*, that we're engaged in the ultimate battle for who shapes Americas ideas, and from what perspective. We are fighting to determine who will decide whether the future of humanity is based upon opportunity, reason, decency, and fairness or upon resentment, anger, hypocrisy, and violence. The choice could not be clearer, but to realize victory in this generational struggle will take all that we can muster.

Chapter 16: The Price of Failure

If you haven't read any of my other books, then you might not know that I aim for two things in all I write: My goals are to be accessible to any intelligent reader who has a broad base of general knowledge, and to impress upon those reading the dangers involved in inaction given the difficulties ahead. The challenge was presented to me to find the pathway forward most likely to lead to the optimal future given our current starting point, and my hope is the preceding chapters have made a compelling and optimistic case for what we can do to assure that our future after Trump is as promising as the hope we feel in this moment. That said, the other thing which I do with no relish is to share the consequences of failure, and so this happy book must end with a most frightful vision of what happens should we fail.

We know the Left has no restraint, and we see indications daily of their spiteful nature and how they plan for the inevitability they believe will soon come when our people, through either complacency or sheer folly, permit them to regain access to the halls of power. Earlier, I repeated my firm conviction that nothing better argues for why we should defeat, demoralize, and marginalize this version of Leftism than their own words, so I will close by giving you a glimpse into what they plan for us all should this unhappy day come to pass, hoping that fright and dismay will serve as motivation to keep us all in the right, remembering that even as these political and cultural struggles are a marathon, that they are also a race we're running with a terrible monster at our backs.

Run too quickly, we exhaust ourselves, and we get caught. Run too slowly, they eclipse us, and swallow us whole. But if we run at just the right pace, hopefully getting more help along the way to aid this quest, then we might just reach the finish where we'll find the weapons with which we can slay this beast, and be safe for a few generations until this ugliness pops up once more in our grandchildren and great-grandchildren who will only have our stories and legends to inform them of the dangers of radical egalitarianism.

While fiction is vivid, I suggest you look into what is presently happening in South Africa or Venezuela as two probable examples of what might be in store for our future if the Marxists are allowed to take control. It may very well sicken you to discover what humanity is capable of, sometimes merely to survive, and how such horrors can be inflicted upon fellow men. These are modern day calamities, perhaps even genocides, but the media ignores them because, as is the case in nearly every circumstance, the Left is the one responsible for the deaths.

Start with South Africa. Thirty years ago, it was a prosperous First World nation, settled by European settlers in an area that was actually less populated by natives than our own North America and whose roots stretch back well over three hundred years. When we hear Africa, we think of Black people and the tribes which primarily inhabit the center of that vast continent, but the reality is that the southern tip of the continent was empty save for a few placid tribes and some nomadic herdsmen. Here, Dutch settlers built their first colony which would eventually, after years of strife and conflict, including the shameful creation of the first concentration camps by their British imperial overlords, emerge as South Africa.

Those same British, who in their ravenous desire to exploit the gold and diamond mines for which South Africa is now famous, imported Africans from Zulu and other tribes to the north of South Africa to undertake the dangerous labor, to displace the native Boers as the Dutch came to be called, and to extract the wealth of their country for their global enterprise. If this sounds like the precursor to the global corporatism which sustains the Left today, you've earned your Rhodes Scholarship as many of the worst ideas were piloted down there.

In response to this, the South African government tried to manage the importation of so many foreigners to their land through the Apartheid regime, which while castigated and demonized by the media, was simply an effort to separate the different groups in society into self-governance. In the same way America was made up of different states like Massachusetts, Pennsylvania, and Virginia, with different peoples and different beliefs, South Africa was also a polyglot state where the British forced together Boer, British, Zulu, and other peoples, each of whom primarily occupied certain areas, and who had different traditions and values.

For as much as it has been derided by those who squawk about equality, the system worked a thousand times better than the current regime in meeting the safety, logistical, and agricultural needs of the people, protecting the rights of the settlers and their private property, a value they brought with them from Europe, but which the radicalized minority groups, who quickly came to be a numerical majority through an extraction driven immigration policy, opposed, because they thought majority rule allowed them to do whatever they wished.

The world agreed with the latter, and celebrated joyously as Nelson Mandela, an avowed communist, came to power in South Africa, marking the end of an era. The old South African flag was erased, the symbols of its history were destroyed, its anthem forbidden, and a new power came to the fore. Twenty-five years have passed: Where are we?

The infrastructure is crumbling, people are seeking to leave in mass exodus even as the government forbids such action, and its major city which literally sits on a river to the ocean is in danger of running out of water. A safe, clean, First World country has now become known for crime, corruption, and in this very year, the government is voting to now legally seize land from families who have worked and held title to it for generations in the name of social justice. Does that sound familiar?

You're not allowed to say this, but the media turns the other way because the crimes are being committed by the Black majority against a White minority. The depressingly commonly occurrence of Boer Farmers being brutally slaughtered after their families are made to watch is covered up by that government, and those who speak out find their lives in peril. These people are not even political, but simply wish to exist and follow the rule of law they had embraced for centuries. Democracy changed that, and a new population meant new laws, with radical Marxist justice having no respect for life, liberty, or property, the foundations upon which South Africa was built just as surely as the United States.

You don't have to believe me. Do your own research and see what happens when nations think they can admit anyone, because we're all good people and those feelings are what count. Besides, equality isn't supposed to mean hurting those who have things, like you probably do if you had the resources to purchase my book. But the funny thing about Marxism is for all their rhetorical talents, and all their theories on redistribution, they don't seem to understand the first bit about why and how people produce things. So, if you do, and you give them power, you had better expect them to use you and abuse you.

If the South African example is disagreeable, consider Venezuela instead. Blessed by proximity to ample oil reserves at a time when prices should have been able to sustain their entire economy despite their socialist leanings, a problem which recurs frequently in Latin America, they invested so poorly and had so much corruption they managed to squander away their wealth to the point where they could not meet their basic needs. I remember reading they reached the point where there was neither food nor toilet paper.

What Hugo Chavez began, and Nicolas Maduro has continued is a government that follows the Castro theory of the state seizing control to help meet the interests of the people. But when people discover that they do not get to keep what they earn, they stop making things and everyone becomes recipients instead of producers. This is the only way Marxism has ever worked, whereby a system promising equality eventually settles in to protect a privileged few, and we see a repeat of Lenin's old dictatorship of the proletariat which sustains the state through increasing violence, force, and corruption. A select few benefit and survive while the remainder of the people, operate at the minimal capacity required to sustain themselves and scrape what they can to survive.

In some ways, Venezuela is simpler and less grotesquely violent than South Africa because unlike the latter, race isn't there to serve to ramp up the violent impulses. Old-school socialism fails in old-school fashion, the same reason why the Soviet Union has now collapsed and why China endures only through embracing nationalist rhetoric heavily beneath its system, which despite being authoritarian, is increasingly capitalist. Even then, however, we see how a billion people live in bondage to that state, and we're seeing its own vulnerabilities become more apparent as America is finally stopping our subsidy of the trade actions through which their state was built, and their economy was financed.

These are but two visions of what the Left might intend. We know they will take away our liberties because they love to censor, ban, and hide our opinions on every platform. We know they want to grab our guns because they fear our ability to resist. We know they will take our wealth because it gives us freedom of action and the ability to exist independently. We know they hate our faith, especially Christianity, because our faith in God is greater than their faith in man. We know that they know, that we are the obstacle standing before their ambition to remake America in their image, and we had better be aware of how far they are willing to go.

The reason the Left has won, in the many cases where they've destroyed otherwise healthy societies is twofold. Divorced from reality, their promise that some government can truly be all things to all people sounds appealing, especially when bolstered by a sycophantic educational system and media. That it is false makes no difference so long as they can siphon wealth from productive people trying to ignore politics and simply live decent lives to create the illusion that their ideas function. When we refuse to confront them and allow them to impose upon us so boldly, we enable their success and our own submission.

Secondly, and more disturbingly, please understand there are no limits to how far they will go to realize their utopia. Consider the case of Josef Stalin, the first true Communist leader to exert control, whose idea of social planning was to kill people at random merely to ensure they didn't get any ideas about resistance. They might have been the lucky ones compared to those sent to the gulags for cause, yet you never hear these stories which were so poignantly told by Solzhenitsyn and others. That's because the Left counts on your own virtue to keep you from believing the depths to which they will go to realize their vision.

These people see Donald Trump as not just a challenge, but an existential threat to their worldview. They interpret our decision to elect him as leader as a declaration of war, especially as we ignored their media, their pundits, their party leadership, and their donors to pronounce our independence. They will punish us, given the opportunity, and give no quarter in how far they will go to make sure another Trump, another nationalist, another patriot is not possible. Such is their vision for after Trump, and it will happen unless we make sure it does not by permanently ensuring these terrible ideas do not destroy America the way they have so many other countries, both great and small.

Epilogue

This book needs no conclusion as the stakes should be clear. We need to ensure the Republican Party works in earnest to develop the nationalist vision which President Trump has begun, and through which we can realize a greater America than ever before. We will have to work hard and hold our fellow citizens to account to accomplish these ends.

The recent loss of the House of Representatives to the Democratic Left in the midterm election only bolsters the argument I've made about their fundamental indecency in the pursuit for power where we saw ballot stuffing in Florida attempt to overturn an election, highly suspect numbers in mail-in ballots in Arizona, and the usual complaints about racial suppression even as voting machines unfailing err only in Democrat favor. They promise gridlock, impeachment, and are emboldened to take the field against us as their cronies in the bureaucracy continue to inhibit the legitimate government's ability to function.

The silver lining is many of the worst Republicans were purged in these defeats, and while this makes for a more dramatic next two years, another opportunity to draw clear distinctions will be coming in 2020, where the re-election of President Trump with an avowedly much more nationalist leaning Congress is not just possible, but necessary. We must work to ensure that happens, to find the right people to support locally, and to continue pushing Trump away from the false promise of moderation for in that path lies our irrevocable demise.

It will take bravery, wisdom, cooperation, patience, and cunning to win the battles ahead. The reality is most people aren't political enough to understand the risks we face and given how much one must understand to be awakened to the potential ramifications, those of us aware must assume an over-sized burden of responsibility until more people come into this great awakening in defense of the American nation.

My conviction is that only nationalism of the strongest and least apologetic variety offers the strength, courage, and resolve necessary to sustain our nation. We will be forced to take new approaches with which many of us will not be comfortable, and to question many of our fundamental assumptions. To care for not just our people, but our most beloved ideas and traditions, we'll have to use government in new ways and understand our opponents better than we ever have before. If we fail to see how they use society and culture against us, our blindness to those attacks will surely result in our eventual defeat and demise.

While the stakes should be much clearer after reading this book, my hope is that you walk away from this not demoralized but rather energized for the fight ahead. We remain the majority as President Trump reminds us, and our movement has both the force and the vision to shape a much better future for America than others intended for us. Whether we achieve that or not will be a question of our dedication and our ability to realize that only we can make it happen.

You know I'll be out there on the front lines. I already have my battle scars from how they scraped me, but it is entirely worth it to imagine a future worth defending. I hope you join me, but more importantly, convince others to support our President and his vision. The day of nationalism has come to America, and where Trump leads, we too shall never tire of winning if we show ourselves willing to learn and to follow.

Acknowledgments

Dana, my beloved wife, has been amazing through these books and these struggles this year, and I am truly blessed to have her in my life. When you live with someone who struggles daily to survive against chronic illness, you learn the true meaning of strength and resiliency and I only hope to live up to her example. I could not be prouder.

We share our Christian faith, with praise for the Lord, Our Savior, and the understanding that through Him all things are possible. In the dark times that preceded Trump, we prayed as many others did for deliverance. Now, in these happier moments, we offer praise and worship in support, with gratitude and vigilance in our hearts. Every man and woman have their own beliefs, but I would say the struggles of this world become much lighter to bear when you understand this life is but a moment in a much larger story.

Taking strong positions cost me many friends and made me powerful enemies, but it has also revealed my truer friends, and they mean so much to us both. For their benefit, I will simply say you know who you are, and we thank you for supporting us. I know that not all share all our beliefs, but there is more to life than politics, and we appreciate that.

However, for those who are allies in the fight, let me say there are no better men than people like John, Bob, Rich, and Hal who have been constant friends and allies, and with whom I am honored to work as we struggle our way toward redemption. I also want to thank the people behind the scenes who support me, knowing I take the charge seriously.

As with every book I write, much of the credit for the final work goes justly to my friend and ally John Young, whose linguistic skills put me to shame, but whose strong prose invariably improves the arguments I try to make but can never get just right. The man is a force of nature, and I thank him profusely, encouraging everyone to check out his independent organization http://www.europeanamericansunited.com.

I want to thank everyone participating in the burgeoning **National Right** movement, an organization based upon common principles of morality, responsibility, liberty, and identity, the counterbalance to the Left. If you're ready to commit to stopping the Left at all costs, we're here when you're ready at https://nationalright.us. More will be coming.

Thanks also to the good men at Pendulum. There might be no less popular cause in America than defending the rights of White people to assert positive identity for themselves, our dreams in the nations our fathers and forefathers built, but there are few less important. When we let the Left divorce us from our kin and our history, we do their work. https://pendulum.online plays an important, if controversial role, in linking our history to our future by asking hard question and dealing with moral quagmires. They make me a better man, and so I offer thanks to Brett, Doug, John, Jeff, Landon, Dustin, Corey, Kenaz, Zorch, Stephen, and Joseph. They are the future, and I'm honored to work with them.

The shock troops remain awesome as always, and I never forget them and their toughness or humor that has gotten me through many a dark mood.

I pride myself on being easy to reach for feedback and fellowship at tom@nationalright.us, so feel free to reach out for any reason. Even if you disagree, I still thank you for taking the time to consider what I have to say, and know I always extend the same courtesy.

Lastly, God bless you, the reader and your family. May the future find you well.

Made in the USA
Middletown, DE
03 May 2019